Insect Eaters

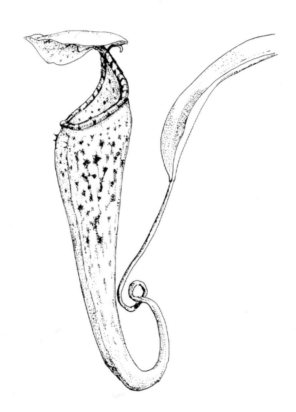

Alphabet and Image Publishers
77 High Street
Totnes
Devon TQ9 5PB

Published by Alphabet and Image Publishers 2006

ISBN 1-899296-30-1
ISBN 978-1-899296-30-9

A CIP catalogue record for this book is available from the British Library.

The publishers and authors disclaim any injury, damage, loss or liability connected with the use of the activities in this book. There may be unintentional errors or ommissions. In this case, please contact the publishers.

Much of this material was first published in hardback in 1986 and in paperback in 1989 by Alphabooks as *Insect Eating Plants and How to Grow Them*.

Printed and bound in China by Compass Press.

Illustrations on page i, iii and vi are:
page i *Nepenthes stenophylla*
page iii *Drosera intermedia*
page vi *S. alata*

Insect Eaters

Adrian Slack

alphabet
&image
PUBLISHERS

Contents

Introduction

Carnivorous plants have been regarded as macabre curiosities of nature-gone-wrong, or less unkindly as science fiction material, interesting enough in its way, but not to be taken very seriously. It was thought that such plants were best confined to the botanic gardens for a rare educational visit. Few imagined that such oddities could be of any horticultural interest, and private collections could be numbered on one hand.

In the US the foundation of *The Carnivorous Plant Newsletter* fanned the flames of public interest, which then spread to Europe and beyond, so that by the time my earlier book *Carnivorous Plants* was first published, general interest had immeasurably increased. *Insect Eaters* does not pretend to be a biology of its subjects – this would have duplicated much of my earlier book. Descriptions, too, when dealing with so many plants, must be brief, but where I felt that one or other plant has particular merit I have indicated this. I hope that the illustrations will go some way towards demonstrating that carnivorous plants are not only an interesting group but that they are almost invariably attractive and that, indeed, some possess beauty to such a degree that their cultivation is well justified for this reason alone.

Adrian Slack

Introducing carnivorous plants

Most insect-eating and other carnivorous plants could correctly be called *insectivorous*, but as others may specialize in catching creatures which are not insects (such a microscopic protozoa and rotifers) the term which I use in this book is *carnivorous*. Surprisingly, there are even those which will supplement their insectivorous diet with small reptiles, scorpions and rodents, which in one species even includes rats!

Almost all carnivorous plants are found in very poor, usually wet soils in which the mineral salts required by most other plants for healthy growth are scarce. Often these are acid boglands on mountains and moorlands, or acid swamps on coastal plains. But many from Australia are found in bushland which is dry for a long time, and here the main growth is usually in the brief period following the rains, when the ground is very wet. The Portuguese Dewy Pine *Drosophyllum* is unusual in favouring poor, dry limestone hillsides, but its extensive root system adapts quite adequately to its water requirements.

There are now fifteen recognized genera of carnivorous plants, divided into over five hundred species. How necessary is this carnivorous diet? It seems to some degree to depend upon the species in question. It is essentially supplementary, for all such plants can take in some nutrients in solution via their root system even if the quantities available are minute, and all absorb carbon dioxide from the air through their leaves, to be broken down to yield carbon and oxygen to manufacture carbohydrates, like other green plants. In Europe and North America you will see thriving colonies of the Round-Leaved Sundew growing on raised floating islands of sphagnum moss in peaty swamps. In the UK, what little nutrient might be contained in the water of the swamp must have been largely removed by the moss, and for these plants the carnivorous diet is clearly of the greatest importance.

Francis Darwin, one of the distinguished sons of the great Victorian naturalist, experimented with this species. He grew two large colonies separately in carefully controlled conditions. In one, each individual was regularly fed with food via its leaves, while those in the other were denied it. Those individuals receiving this food thrived, while the others were noticeably less vigorous, producing fewer flowers and less seed. He concluded that the latter plants, if perpetually deprived of their carnivorous diet, would be less able to compete with other plants and that this would ultimately lead to their extinction.

Massive plants of one pitcher plant – the Huntsman's Cup *Sarracenia purpurea* ssp. *purpurea* – are often found on sphagnum islands of the type described above.

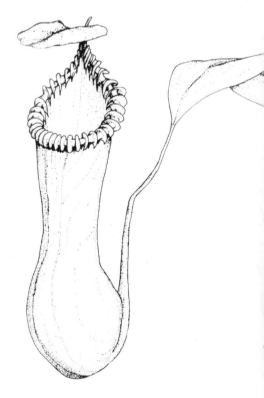

N. edwardsiana lower pitcher

The Northern Pitcher plant *S. purpurea ssp. purpurea*

At the other extreme there are species in which the supplementary diet seems much less important. Thus *Pinguicula moranensis*, a butterwort from Central America, thrives in cultivation even when deprived of flies, while there is a wild form of an Australian Sundew, *Drosera erythrorhiza*, which has tentacles and is deprived of any means of catching insects, yet it is as vigorous as those which do; it is possible that those with tentacles are better equipped to grow in poorer soils.

Carnivorous plants have been in cultivation for at least 340 years, though their carnivorous nature was not suspected for the greater part of that time.

John Tradescant, head gardener to King Charles I, had the Huntsman's Cup *Sarracenia purpurea* in cultivation in 1640, which he had probably brought with him from Virginia in 1637. The following century saw the introduction of the Yellow Trumpet *Sarracenia flava*, the Sweet Trumpet *Sarracenia rubra*, the Assam Monkey Cup *Nepenthes khasians*, and *Nepenthes ampullaria*.

The nineteenth century was the heyday of the great conservatories and stovehouses, both in Europe and North America. Plant rarities from all over the world were eagerly sought after for collections by the landed and the wealthy, and in this way an increasing number of carnivorous plants found their way into cultivation. In the first half of that century the Fork-Leaved Sundew *Drosera binata* made its appearance, and amongst other newcomers were the White Trumpet *Sarracenia leucophylla*, the Hooded Trumpet *Sarracenia minor*, and the little Western Australian Pitcher plant *Cephalotus follicularis*. The second part of the century was notable for the large number of Monkey Cup *Nepenthes* species introduced, from which many fine and often spectacular hybrids were raised.

Disaster struck European collections in 1914 with the First World War. As a result of fuel restrictions it became no longer possible to heat the great glasshouses which had been created for these collections. It marked the end of an era. Almost overnight great plant collections ceased to exist. The period between the First World War and the 1950s saw interest in carnivorous plants at its lowest ebb. The 1950s saw a slight revival of interest in Britain, but enthusiasm in Japan was greater, and this soon led to the founding of the Carnivorous Plant Society of Japan. Gradually more and more species found their way back into cultivation. In 1972 two American enthusiasts, Dr Donald E. Schnell and Mr Joseph Mazrimas, published the first English language journal on the subject, *The Carnivorous Plant Newsletter*. This is still the journal of the International Carnivorous Plant Society, and it did more than anything else to foster initial interest in the plants, not only in North America but in Europe, Australia, New Zealand and other countries.

With their increasing popularity, new and improved techniques of cultivating carnivorous plants have evolved, and the majority of the species can be grown with a minimum of effort. Many are indeed amenable to cultivation at home, a fact which our Victorian predecessors might have found hard to believe.

The traps themselves can be conveniently divided into two groups: 'passive' and 'active'. The passive traps catch their victims with glue-like mucilage, as flypaper does, or they use the slippery pitfall method which we see in the pitcher plants. A third type makes use of the 'lobster pot' technique, in which the victim enters a chamber through a tubular entrance which it cannot re-find, as in the Parrot Pitcher plant. With active traps, the sundews first detain their prey with sticky-glanded tentacles, but as the creature struggles surrounding tentacles bend over the victim, overwhelming it with sticky secretion. In many species the leaf blade itself is then brought into action, folding around the victim's body to aid the digestive process.

A technique similar to the spring trap is seen in the well-known Venus Fly Trap, in which two leaf lobes close quickly together, while in the bladderworts we see a method which is somewhat reminiscent of an old-fashioned mousetrap. When a small swimming organism accidentally touches a trigger device it causes a trapdoor to open. The victim is sucked immediately through this doorway by the release of a partial vacuum and the door then instantly closes behind it.

Digestion is at its simplest in the Sun Pitcher plants: by bacterial activity in water, the nutrients which are released into solution are absorbed into the plant's system. However, in most species it is achieved in a more sophisticated way by means of digestive enzymes and acid secreted by the plant, bacteria also playing a greater or lesser part in the process in many species.

Once a few elementary procedures are understood most of these plants are very easily cultivated. In fact, a number make excellent and undemanding subjects for sunny window-sills, providing never-failing sources of interest and beauty, while some actually double as first-rate housefly controls. Unfortunately, cultivation failures are numerous. Some such cases are undoubtedly caused by the shockingly poor material still too readily available at many shops and garden centres; but perhaps many more are caused by lack of information on cultivation, not helped by often inadequate or incomplete instructions supplied with the plants. A further stumbling block is caused by the fact that the techniques for successful cultivation are quite different from those needed by the common run of houseplants, so that the chance of guessing it correctly without previous information is remote, and a dead plant does not get a second chance! I hope this book will go some way towards resolving this problem, and as the death-roll of Venus Fly Traps probably exceeds all others, I decided to describe the cultivation of this plant first.

The Venus Fly Trap

Seen in action for the first time, this fly trap is amazing. Whether or not you want to grow this plant, this chapter will tell you how to look after the Venus Fly Trap, *Dionaea muscipula*, successfully, and you will then have the main key to the cultivation of many other carnivorous plants described in the following chapters.

The leaf blade consists of two lobes edged with prong-like teeth. Within their margins is a narrow area baited with nectar which attracts the prey, while in the centre of each blade are several trigger hairs. Touch one hair once and there is no reaction. Touch it twice, or another hair once, and the trap will close, often with surprising speed. This is one of those plants that is very easy to grow, but only if

Dionaea muscipula with two unsuspecting visitors

you know the right method. Follow these instructions 'to the letter', and you should succeed.

Cultivation To grow your plant in the house or in a conservatory or greenhouse, the method is virtually the same. The position is important, for it must be sunny. Always choose a window-sill which gets plenty of sun, preferably south-facing, and place the plant as close to the glass as possible. Temperature is less important than is often thought. Your fly trap will appreciate high temperatures in summer, but any ordinary room temperature is satisfactory. It likes to be kept cooler if possible in winter, so move it into the window of a cooler room, though this is not vital.

Root run is another vital consideration. A healthy plant will develop a surprisingly long root system, and will not thank you if this is cramped. Even well-grown plants on the market are usually in pots which are on the small side, so repotting is advisable for your plant to thrive. This must only be done in spring or summer when it is in full growth, and never in autumn or winter. As a rough guide, if the traps are less than 12mm (0.5in) long the plant can stay in a 75–100mm (3–4in) pot; if longer, choose either a 130mm (5in) dwarf plastic pot or a 115mm (4.5in) one. Not all manufacturers make these exact sizes, but you should be able to obtain very similar pots.

To remove the plant from the pot without damaging its roots, turn the pot upside down and carefully apply one or more hard knocks to its edge against a hard object, such as the side of a bench, and allow the plant with its roots and compost intact to fall gently into the palm of your other hand. Correct compost is also vital. Only one mixture is satisfactory, and perhaps it is not surprising that this happens to be similar to the soil in which the plant grows in its natural habitat in the North and South Carolinas, in the US. Add two parts of granulated moss peat to one part of horticultural sand and mix well.

Plants bought from shops and garden centres often appear to prosper for a period, only to decline and die later. So if your plant appears to have been potted in a different medium and it is spring or summer, repot it and tease away as much of the old compost as you can as gently as possible, so as not to damage the roots. It is easiest to do this if you place the unpotted plant under water, for the old compost will then come away easily. If your plant has already been potted in the correct mixture, do not remove before repotting into a larger pot.

Potting should be carried out with care. Crocks are not required at the bottom, but place a very little moss or root fibre over the drainage holes to avoid any escape of compost. Put sufficient mixture in the pot to fill it by about a third, and press this down very firmly with your fingers so as to allow no air spaces. Check that this allows adequate room for your plant. If bare-rooted, see that the main roots run downwards and slightly outwards (i.e. do not double them back on themselves), and that the crown of the plant is about 6mm (0.25 inch) below the rim of the pot. Now run more compost among and around the roots, gently firming with your fingers as you go so that no air pockets are left, finally firming all of it. The crown should be in the centre of the pot, and all its green part should be exposed, while all the creamy-whitish part must be submerged. If your plant is not bare-rooted but in its compost from the previous pot or container, things are more simple. Just put sufficient compost at the base to raise it to the necessary level, allowing for firming, and run compost around the sides, firming well, while seeing that the crown is in the centre of the pot. A light sprinkling from the watering-can will clean up the plant and settle the surface of the compost.

Watering Like most other carnivorous plants, the Venus Fly Trap is a bog plant, so its watering requirements are quite different from other houseplants. It is necessary to ensure that the compost is always wet so, permanently stand the pot in about 12–25mm (0.5–1in) of water. This must be soft water, for hard water is poisonous to this and, indeed, to most other carnivorous plants. Collected rain, distilled or deionized water are all suitable. So, too, is the water left from defrosting the fridge (not from ice-cubes), but never use water from a conventional water-softener for it contains salt, which is also poisonous to these plants.

The saucer, tray or plant trough containing water should be a good deal wider than the pot to allow adequate local humidity around the plant, but this has the added advantage that the water-supply lasts longer than in a narrower vessel. If you use one of the saucers made by pot manufacturers to match their pots, this should be up to two sizes larger than the size intended for that pot.

Care After potting-on a fly trap which is already rooted in its own compost, no precautions are needed to re-establish the plant. However, if it was bare-footed give it a period of special care. Immediately after placing the pot in shallow water cover it with an inverted drinking glass or propagator cover, to cut down transpiration and encourage re-establishment of the roots.

The plant must be shaded from direct sunlight during that time to prevent it from becoming 'stewed'. Remove the glass after a week to ten days, and continue shading for about three days longer, as a precaution against shock, before being removed. It is often thought that these plants should be kept permanently under some such propagating cover, but never do this. Excessive humidity is unnecessary and can lead to sappy weak growth, and these covers will keep out the flies that the plant must catch if it is to thrive.

PESTS AND DISEASES

Fortunately these are few. Of pests, the only one likely to prove troublesome is greenfly (*Aphis*), which are too small to be caught and hardly affect the mature growth. They often attack the centre of the crowns in early spring where they are largely hidden from view, but their presence becomes apparent when distorted traps are produced as a result of their activity.

If the plant is well established and in reasonably good health, an easy way of removing greenflies is to submerge the entire plant in a bucket of soft water for three days, repeating the process a second time about a week after removing the

Above: Inside the open trap of *Dionaea muscipula*

Far right: Spectacular red coloration of traps of young plants

pot from the water. Alternatively, you may spray the plant with almost any approved houseplant aphicide or general houseplant insecticide.

Diseases Grey Mould (*Botrytis cinerea*) can occasionally be a problem. This resembles the type of mould found on old bread. It is almost always caused by poor hygiene or poor light, and should not occur if you have removed dead growth and have your plant in a sunny position. It usually starts on dead growth, spreading to and killing live tissue. All dead and apparently affected growth should be removed and the plant should then be sprayed with a good systematic fungicide, such as Benlate.

Bacterial rot can cause roots to die, often resulting in the death of the plant, but again this is almost invariably the result of faulty cultivation. It is often caused by incorrect watering, by too small a pot restricting the root system, and by the use of soil fertilizer. Possible symptoms are yellowing, floppy or distinctly unhealthy-looking foliage. If your plant is not too badly affected it can often be revived by thoroughly washing what may be left of the root system, soaking for a few minutes in Benlate solution mixed as for a spray, and repotting into a sufficiently larger pot in new compost.

Propagation There are three methods – division, leaf cuttings or seed. Of these, the simplest is division, but you must wait for two or three years until the plant has formed a clump consisting of four or five crowns. Dividing it earlier than this is often possible, but over-frequent division tends to inhibit the plant's development. Unpot the plant and free the roots of compost in a bucket of water, as explained earlier. If it is ready for division you will find that it breaks apart almost naturally into two or more pieces.

Leaf cuttings are best taken in early spring, and not later than mid-summer. You need a supply of green live sphagnum moss – no other moss is suitable. First remove the plant from its pot and wash it, so that the entire leaf can be removed back to its base beneath the compost surface. Pull off manually, remove any jagged edge by a neat cut with a razor blade. Cut the trap cleanly and discard, use only the leaf. Then employ exactly the same technique for sundew leaf cuttings described on page 24, being careful to ensure that the upper surface of the stalk faces uppermost. One leaf usually produces from one to several plants, which generally take twelve to eighteen months to reach maturity. When the young plants have developed good root systems they should be separated if too close together and numerous, but most can be left in their container until they are nearly mature, when they should be potted.

Seed raising is the least satisfactory of the three methods of propagation, for the seedlings are slow to reach maturity, often taking five years, and seed is sparsely produced. Use the same method described for sundews on page 24, pricking the seedlings out when large enough to handle into a seed box, spacing them about 3cm (1.2in) apart.

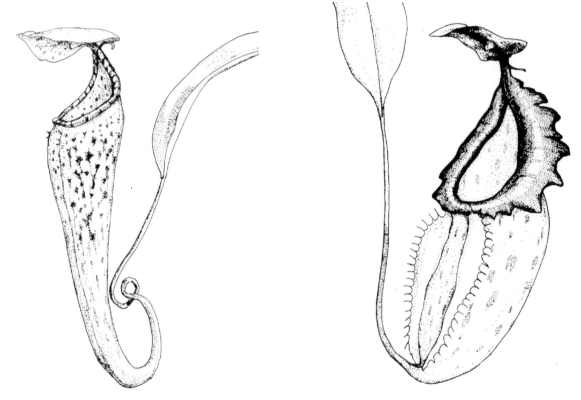

Cultivation: the main points

Above: *Nepenthes stenophylla,* an upper pitcher
Above right: An upper pitcher of the hybrid *Nepenthes x tiveyi*

Select plants with a critical eye, or purchase by mail order from a reputable grower. Buy, whenever possible, during the growing season. It is not only more exciting to see your plants in full growth, but it is psychologically important, for it will give you the confidence that you can grow them. Buy fully grown material; the price may be higher, but the risk of losing them is so much less.

There is a wide range of attractive and exciting species which can be grown in sunny windows, using methods very similar to the cultivation of the Venus Fly Trap, and taken one step further with the addition of electric lighting and of a terrarium. Growing a collection principally or entirely under glass widens your choice of plants, and unless you wish to grow tropicals such as the lowland *Nepenthes,* your first choice is likely to be for a cool greenhouse that is easily heated and maintained, and in it you can grow well over half the carnivorous plant species in cultivation. Some species are frost hardy and may be grown out of doors in temperate climates in specially constructed artificial bogs or frames. But whatever you use, please read the section 'At Home' page 8, first, for it will throw more light on the general requirements of your plants.

Water As emphasised on page 3, hard water containing lime is poisonous to almost all carnivorous plants. Never use it unless otherwise stated in this book. Public supply, or 'mains' water, in most areas contains lime; also often the case with pond water, and usually so with river water. If in doubt, test it with a pH-testing solution available from chemists and drug stores. Suitable sources of soft water are collected rain, distilled water and deionized water. You may also use the water left after defrosting the fridge, but note that frozen lime-containing water (i.e. ice-cubes) contains just as much lime and is just as poisonous on melting. Water from the conventional water-softener is also often poisonous, due to the presence of salt, and must not be used.

If you live in a hard-water area in which the mains water contains lime, and you require fairly large quantities of soft water, there is a simple way to make the lime inactive by the use of dilute sulphuric acid at 10 per cent strength. But never handle the concentrated acid unless you are qualified to do so. This is one of the most dangerous acids known, and accidental mishandling can too easily lead to an explosion, loss of eyesight, and grievous bodily injury. Better to order from your pharmacist as a 10 per cent solution; this is relatively slow in reaction and therefore fairly safe to handle if treated with care. All the same, your eyes should be protected with goggles, and if spilt on bare hands the acid should be washed off to avoid burns. Keep it away from clothing, too. You will also need a graduated measuring cylinder of about 25ml, a water pH-testing kit, and a water tank of suitable size for your requirements. Fill the tank with mains water and test its pH. If hard, the indicator will show a number higher than neutral (7.0 pH). The water should be on the acid side of neutral, ie. 6.5pH or just below. Assuming that this is not the case, now add 10ml of the 10 per cent acid. Mix well, and note the pH. You may need to do this a number of times before 6.5pH is reached. Take note of how many ml of acid you have needed to adjust the pH, for, assuming that the alkalinity of your mains water is not subject to variation (unlikely), this will be the probable quantity you will need each time the tank is refilled.

Fertilizers With the exception of *Nepenthes* do not apply fertilizers of any kind in the soils of carnivorous plants. Remember that these are plants of naturally poor soils. Fertilizers will sour the compost and cause the roots to rot. Even indoors your plants should catch sufficient prey for their needs, but if you are in doubt you may safely give them a fortnightly spray with quarter-strength fertilizer solution, as directed for *Nepenthes* (see page 125), in spring or summer only.

Light The individual requirements for light and shade vary among the species, but are of great importance. If you try to grow your Trumpet Pitcher plants in shade they will not only become drawn and weak, but sooner or later you are likely to lose them due to fungoid or bacterial attack; while if you expose your

Mexican Butterworts to strong sunlight in a greenhouse, the leaves will become yellowish and may be subject to leaf burn.

Compost material Choose the ingredients for your potting mixtures with care. Peat must always be granulated moss peat. Never use sedge peat, which is quite unsuitable for these plants. It has the wrong consistency, can be alkaline and poisonous. Sand should be good, washed, horticultural sand, bought from a garden centre or nursery. It must be sharp, but not too coarse (so avoid grits and gypsum), and free from chalk and shells. Sand from the beach and builders' sand must never be used. Perlite must be of a type intended for horticulture or it may contain poisonous impurities. Bark should always be purchased from a reputable supplier to orchid growers, or from an orchid nursery. Do not harvest your own! Sphagnum moss should be live unless otherwise stated in this book, and of a succulent, open kind; aquatic kinds are unsuitable. This moss is often difficult to obtain, and must not be taken from the wild except with the landowner's or farmer's permission. Some nurseries will supply it, and *Darlingtonia* will often be supplied ready-established in live sphagnum. Please note that ordinary non-sphagnum mosses cannot be used, and would kill your plants. John Innes Compost No.2 is available commercially in some countries, or you can mix it yourself. The useful constituents are the sterilized loam, the base fertilizer and chalk, not the peat and sand. It consists of 7 parts sterilized granulated loam, 3 parts granulated moss peat, 2 parts horticultural sand, and to each cubic yard (0.7m^3) of this mixture is added 4.5kg (10lb) John Innes Base Fertilizer, and 910g (2lb) ground chalk. The base fertilizer is made of 2 parts by weight of hoof and horn, 2 parts super phosphate of lime, and 1 part sulphate of potash. Alternatively, a good loam-based, houseplant potting compost should be acceptable. Before mixing your composts, check that all lumps have been broken up; these are likely to occur in the peat.

AT HOME

Even if you grow the majority of your plants under glass you can also be successful with those you grow indoors. A number make excellent subjects for the window-sill. The majority of these are simpler to grow than the average houseplant, and unlike the latter you cannot easily over water them. Amongst those that I shall recommend are some of the most beautiful of all carnivorous plants, one of which – the Yellow Trumpet – doubles as the most effective housefly control I know of, and should be in every house for that reason alone.

The general method for indoor cultivation is extremely simple. Pot up your plant in the compost advised in the section of the book dealing with that species, then stand it in 12–25mm (0.5–1in) of soft water, just as was recommended for the Venus Fly Trap. The water container can be a plant-pot saucer two sizes larger than the pot itself, or for several plants, a narrow plant tray or plant trough free of drainage holes may be better. It is best to use simple plant troughs just deep enough to conceal the sides of the pots. Whichever container you use, the important points are that it should be sufficiently wide to cope with the water requirements of the plants over a period, and at the same time provide a permanent humidity around them. Hygiene is as important as in the greenhouse, so remove all dead and diseased leaves and growth. Pests are rare, but outbreaks of aphis are usually easily controlled with an approved houseplant aphicide.

The majority of suitable species are sun-lovers and all these are best grown at south-facing windows, close to the glass. Insufficient light leads to weak, drawn-out growth which is unattractive, and all too often leads to disease and death.

STARTING OUT

If you are a beginner, start with one of the North American Trumpet Pitcher plants, *Sarracenia*. The Yellow Trumpet *Sarracenia flava*, combines great beauty with interest, and it keeps the flies down. An easy plant, but so is the Huntsman's Cup *S. purpurea venosa*, the Green Trumpet *S. oreophila*, and the hybrids *S. x catesbaei* and *S. x melanorhoda*. Curiously, the Parrot Pitcher *S. psittacina* will do well, too, without any need to apply the immersion technique when grown under glass. Other *Sarracenia* species require more light than is normally available in all but the sunniest windows. Their exciting relative, the Cobra Lily *Darlingtonia californica*, will thrive here also, providing its special watering requirements are catered for.

You can grow sundews species which form flat rosettes, excluding Australian tuberous species and those that form winter resting buds. Especially suitable are all *Drosera spatulata* forms, *D. aliciae, D. dielsiana, D. montana, D. humiltonii,* and the more vigorous pygmies including *D. pulchella* forms and *D.* sp. 'Bannister'. Those species that have upright to semi-upright leaves are unsuitable, for while leaves held closely to the ground experience a high enough local humidity to support adequate drops of mucilage, upright leaves are held above this zone and do not.

Of the beautiful butterworts of Central America all forms of *Pinguicula moranensis* are suitable for you to grow, as are many of the hybrids, including 'Sethos', 'Weser', 'Tina' and *x kewensis*. Their distant cousins, the terrestrial bladderworts, often make good window plants too, perhaps one of the loveliest being the almost continuously flowering and delicately pretty *Utricularia sandersonii*.

Fewer species will grow successfully on east and west-facing sills. In good, unbroken light the Trumpet Pitcher plants *Sarracenia purpurea venosa, S. psittacina* and *S. x catesbaei* will succeed, as will *Darlingtonia*, while the butterworts and terrestrial bladderworts already listed will grow reasonably well. On north-facing sills you are severely limited. Here terrestrial bladderworts will succeed, while the Waterwheel plant *Aldrovanda* and the aquatic bladderworts will succeed in glass bowls and aquaria.

Artificial light To grow your plants indoors, but in places in which there is insufficient or no light, you can do so under fluorescent lighting. There are a number of small units on the market designed specially for the purpose, or you

Above: The Alice Sundew *Drosera aliciae*

Below: A large fly on the Yellow Trumpet *Sarracenia flava*

Sarracenia flava

may rig up your own to suit your needs, in which case note that the fluorescent control gear must be housed separately in dry conditions, and that the electrical installation must be checked by a qualified electrician before use. The tubes should provide sufficient light in the red and blue wavelengths, so use either a true Daylight Tube or the special 'Gro-Lux' type.

Wherever possible use twin-tube units complete with reflectors, for without the latter your plants will lose a lot of light. The tubes can be suspended over a 'growing table', or you can construct lighted shelves for a larger collection. There is not normally room for reflectors in a shelving system, so the underside of each upper shelf and the inner side of the pelmet which conceals the light tube should be painted white to reflect as much light as possible.

For healthy growth plants do need to be rather nearer to the light tubes than is generally realized. *Pinguicula*, *Drosera* and terrestrial *Utricularia* all need to be within 30cm (12in) of the tubes, while *Sarracenias* should be even nearer – within about 15cm (6in). The difficulty of accommodating the tall-pitchered species is obvious, and this can only be done satisfactorily with a banked arrangement of about four tubes, but lighting from above will be found suitable for decumbent-leaved kinds such as *SS. purpurea venosa, psittacina, x melanorhoda, x courtii* and *x wrigleyana*. Switch on the lights for sixteen hours a day in summer, gradually lowering it to about nine hours in winter, gradually raising this again in spring to reach the sixteen hours by the summer. A twenty-four hour timeswitch is handy.

The terrarium For a minority of carnivorous plants a highly humid climate is best if they are to thrive, while for a few it is essential. Of occasional use in the greenhouse, the home terrarium provides the most attractive and easily managed growing environment. It can be no more than a glass or plastic case on a waterproof tray, with some ventilation. It may be unheated, relying on your room temperature for its heat source, and this will normally be suitable for plants requiring cool greenhouse temperatures. Or you can heat it to grow those needing tropical rainforest conditions.

Unheated terrariums You can make an unheated terrarium simply by placing a loose sheet of glass over an aquarium. The sheet must be slightly overlapping on all sides of the aquarium, and it may be slightly moved to one side if ventilation is required, but this is very seldom needed in practice, unless the unit is exposed to strong sunlight. The chief advantage of the aquarium model is that you may make it almost any size to suit the plants you grow. However commercially produced models are available. The larger rectangular models sold as propagators are ideal, and although their heights are somewhat restricted most terrarium-suitable plants are smaller. Avoid unventilated structures known as Wardian Cases – miniature greenhouses with leaded lights – and bottle gardens, as these are quite unsuitable.

In an unheated terrarium your plants may be grown either in pots or in a specially prepared bed. You may prefer the pots rather than the base of the terrarium being used as a water tray, or sand bed saturated with water to. But the bed method does allow you to develop your own ideas in landscaping, and is good for allowing natural colonizers such as *Cephalotus* and *Drosera prolifera* to spread. You will need to place on the bottom a 13mm (0.5in) layer of coarse horticultural Perlite or lime-free gravel. Cover this with the thinnest possible barrier layer of sphagnum moss or root fibre. Now fill the remainder of the tray with a mixture of 3 parts moss peat to 1 part horticultural sand to within about 13mm (0.5in) of the top. Plant up and water judiciously with the sprinkler on the can, so that the compost is wet rather than a swamp. A useful device is a 40mm (1.6in) diameter plastic tube inserted to the full depth at one corner. Water is fed into the tray via the tube until the required saturation is achieved. Ideally no water should be visible at the bottom of the tube after watering. A little will not matter, but 25mm (1in) or more indicates over-watering. Loss of vapour through the ventilators is so slight that you will seldom find it necessary to water again for several weeks or longer.

Of electrically heated structures, otherwise known as heated propagators. There is a wide range. Disregard price if you can, and simply go for excellence, for a faulty cable or thermostat may spell death to your plants. The temperature range should not be less than 7–30°C (45–85°F). Choose one of the larger models if you intend to grow *Nepenthes*.

Heated terrariums In a heated terrarium a different method is used. In most models 13mm (0.5in) or more of sand is placed over the bottom, according to the manufacturer's instructions, and this is kept permanently moist by occasional application of soft water. The bed method is therefore impractical and the plants must be grown in pots. Tropical *Drosera*, *Pinguicula*, and terrestrial and epiphytic *Utricularia* can be watered on the tray system, but as their compost will remain wet for weeks it is unnecessary to keep water standing in the trays or saucers permanently. However, *Nepenthes*, which require ultra-sharp drainage, must never be watered on this system but always from above. If you place a shallow layer of finely broken live sphagnum over the compost surface of these plants, this soon grows, and when watering becomes necessary every few days this is indicated by a noticeable lightening of the colour of the moss. It also prevents erosion of the compost during watering.

Where light is poor suspend two fluorescent electric light tubes complete with reflector directly over the top of the terrarium. Choose a light tube as near as you can to the length of the terrarium you wish to illuminate. If the top is plastic see that the tube is not near enough to overheat, soften and distort. (For further details see the section on artificial light starting on page 9.) Specially made units to fit some models are now available.

HAZARDS
Good hygiene is of particular importance in the enclosed conditions of the terrarium. Here fungus diseases in particular would find an ideal breeding ground, so remove all dead and diseased foliage and growth. Access to pests is largely barred by the glass, but they can be imported with new plants, compost materials and pots. Aphis may be troublesome, but are easily controlled with most approved houseplant insecticides. Algae sometimes form on the inner sides of the glass as a green film, but can be removed with a soft cloth damped with detergent solution. Moss can be attractive, but its growth may get out of hand, especially around small plants, when it can easily be clipped back with scissors.

SUITABLE PLANTS
The Western Australian Pitcher plant *Cephalotus follicularis*, will thrive on a problematical north-facing or sunless window-sill, providing there is sufficient light. So, too, will the three exciting Queensland Sundews (see page 35). For south, west, and east-facing window-sills the lovely orchid-flowered epiphytic bladderworts of South America are a good choice. They like a little sun, which will encourage them to produce their magnificent flowers, but try to avoid prolonged strong sunlight which can burn their foliage. *Cephalotus* will thrive here,

the pitchers colouring more vividly where exposed to plenty of sunlight. Many sundews with erect or semi-erect foliage unsuitable for open window-sill culture will succeed in the terrarium providing it is placed in a really sunny south-facing window or, alternatively, is well lit with a fluorescent light unit. The Cape Sundew *Drosera capensis*, and the Fork-Leaved Sundews (see pages 28 and 33), are amongst the most suitable. Also good window-sill plants Central American butterworts, which are forms of *Pinguicula moranensis*, thrive especially well in the terrarium, often producing extra lush foliage. They need a southern aspect or fluorescent light, but prolonged strong sunlight may cause leaf burn. Providing your terrarium is large enough, and the summer and winter room temperature ranges are within those recommended, you may even be able to grow one or two of the highland *Nepenthes* referred to below, of which *N. alata* is one of the most tolerant and easy.

Temperatures Both highland and lowland *Nepenthes* come into their own in a heated terrarium, the limiting factors being available space and choice of temperature. They make attractive and extraordinarily interesting subjects, simple to cope with providing you choose small growers or those of the more robust species which are tolerant of frequent pruning. In this way you may house as many as six plants in a 76 x 41 x 43cm (30 x 16 x 17in) model. All require a good light with some sun, otherwise they should be lit by fluorescent tubes. Exceptions are the *N. rafflesiana* forms, *N. ampullaria* and *N. x hookeriana*, which will all happily produce their pitchers in sunless, but moderately well-lit conditions.

Lowland species require a constant summer temperature of 22–26°C (71–79°F), and a constant winter one of 21°C (71°F). For highland species, which are used to cooler day temperatures and often chilly nights, it is best to vary the summer temperature accordingly to 20°C (68°F) by day, 14°C (57°F) by night, and in winter 12.5°C (55°F) by day, and a minimum of 10°C (50°F) by night. In practice your daily routine may make this difficult to arrange, and a constant summer temperature of 18.5°C (65°F) and a winter one of 10°C (50°F) minimum will usually suffice.

A number of highland species will adapt to lowland temperatures and can therefore be mixed with lowland species, examples being *NN. alata, ventricosa, fusca, stenophylla, x ventrata,* and, strangely, *N. lowii*. In contrast, lowland species will not thrive for long in the conditions recommended for highlanders. Of these, suitable plants are the *N. ampullaria, N. gracilis* and *N. rafflesiana* forms, *NN. x trichocarpa, x hookeriana, x boissiense* and *x. boissiense rubra*. In addition to the highlanders listed above, two excellent terrarium plants are *NN. gymnamphora* and *tentaculata*, each retaining a semi-dwarf habit for a considerable time, although unlike those plants neither is tolerant of excessively high temperatures.

The Queensland Sundews will grow rather more vigorously in the heated than in the unheated terrarium, and seem unconcerned about temperature providing the winter minimum is not below 10°C (50°F). The same can be said of most or perhaps all the Central American butterworts, with the exception of the cool-tolerant *Pinguicula moranensis* forms and their hybrids. The dwarf species, such as *PP. cyclosecta, ehlersae* and *esseriana*, make delightful subjects for smaller terrariums. Here you may also grow sub-tropical and tropical species of terrestrial and epiphytic *Utricularia*, such as *UU. caerulea, spiralis, dichotoma* and *montana*.

THE GREENHOUSE

The great majority of carnivorous plants will mix well with other greenhouse plants providing their individual requirements are met. The site should be level, in the sunniest position possible, and not exposed to strong, especially cold, winds. The house should be well built and strong, metal being longer-lasting than wood. Polythene tunnels are sometimes used, but winter heat losses are considerable compared with glass, and the covers have to be renewed biennially. Avoid choosing too small a house if you can – collections have a habit of expanding rapidly! It should be at least 2.4m (7ft10in) wide, but preferably 3m (10ft) since this allows room for a path 91cm (3ft) wide.

A path is best made of concrete non-slip slabs or of flooring bricks, both of which provide good surfaces for walking on and 'damping down'. The roof vents should be automatically operated vent openers (because of the possibility of power cuts); those operating by chemical expansion are best. Rainwater is valuable and should be collected from the roof by guttering and ducted to adequate storage butts. These should be located outside the house, with the possible exception of the stovehouse (see page 16). There should be staging on either side of the path. This must be absolutely level if the tray system of watering is to be used; to ensure this, a spirit-level or tray of shallow water should be used during installation. For the same reason the staging legs must be prevented from gradually sinking under the weight while they must support, and must stand upon secure bases such as paving slabs on consolidated ground.

Every house must have a maximum-minimum thermometer within, and to ensure accurate readings this must be placed in a completely sunless position away from heat sources or cold draughts. In the colder months it should be read and reset every morning.

Watering The tray system is by far the most suitable for the large majority of

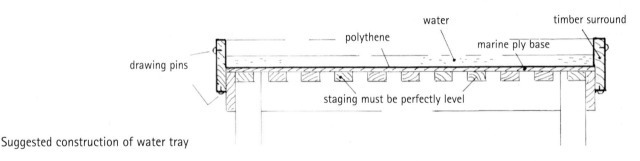

Suggested construction of water tray

carnivorous plants, with some exceptions such as *Nepenthes* and *Drosophyllum*. This is the simplest and least time-consuming system, yet provides ideally moist root conditions and humidity for healthy growth. You will need a horizontal tray 4–5cm (1.5–2in) deep. From spring to autumn you would normally maintain about 2.5cm (1in) of soft water in this. The plants stand in this in their pots or similar containers. If you go away for a week you may completely fill the tray with water, and this will usually last for at least that period in warm weather. However, in winter too much humidity combined with wetness can encourage Grey Mould (*Botrytis*) on some plants, so it is best to leave the trays dry most of the time, periodically pouring in sufficient water for the pots to fully absorb so that the compost is kept moist but no water remains in the tray.

Use greenhouse gravel trays, leaving out the gravel, or make your own. If you make your own it is easily done to fit the staging. If the staging is of the open, slatted kind, first cover this over with rot-proof marine plywood. Make the sides of the trough with a timber surround freestanding to the desired height (see diagram page 14), and make waterproof with a liner of heavy-gauge black polythene. In calculating the size of this sheet, allow not only for the base and sides but extra for folding over the latter and securing. For neatness allow sufficient on the tray's visible side to be secured just beneath the side of the staging, as shown.

Shading Most carnivorous plants are sun loving, but with very few exceptions most of these dislike very strong sunlight under greenhouse conditions. In some this will cause yellowing of the foliage, or even leaf burn. Some degree of shading is therefore necessary during summer. Slatted roller shades or simple green shade netting may be used, but preferably brush-on or spray-on shading on the outer surface of the glass, applied to the density required. It must be removed in the autumn, when it is easily washed off.

Types of greenhouse Carnivorous plants come from a wide variety of climates. At one extreme are plants from mountains in temperate regions, which may experience continuous frost in winter; at the other, plants from sweltering tropical rainforests. Fortunately the majority come between these two extremes and may be accommodated easily in what we call the cool greenhouse or coolhouse. If planning a mixed collection, such a house would be a wise choice. But if you wish to put up more than one type of greenhouse it is advisable to include these in a single range if this proves practical, for in this way you will economize to some degree both on heating and on glasshouse cost. From the point of view of heat preservation, the following arrangements are sensible.

For a range consisting of a coolhouse and a stovehouse, have the outside entrance on the coolhouse with an internal door leading into the stovehouse. For one consisting of a coolhouse, stovehouse and warmhouse, again have outside entry into the coolhouse, with an internal door into the stovehouse, and one from the stovehouse into the warmhouse. If you wish to include a coldhouse too, this

PARAFFIN HEATING
PROS: cheap heaters are inexpensive and simple to maintain
CONS: cannot be thermostatically controlled
Sulphur fumes could be toxic to some plants *(Heliamphora)*
Ventilation essential at all times when the heaters are in use

GAS HEATING
PROS: gas heaters can be thermostatically controlled
Do not emit toxic fumes
CONS: essential to use a non-toxic gas
Ventilation essential at all times
Most sources of natural gas are safe, including North Sea gas in Britain, and the bottled gas propane

ELECTRICAL TUBULAR OR FAN HEATERS
PROS: no fumes
No use of oxygen
In greenhouses it takes the form of tubular or fan heaters
Good for a stovehouse in a frost-free country
CONS: the very real risk of power cuts or failure make their use inadvisable
Cost of installing a power-failure alarm
Cost of alternative heating system i.e. a generator

SOLID FUEL
Not recommended because labour intensive
The cost of coal continues to rise
Expensive to install
Most need electric pumps or fans, which will cease to function during power failure

The Tall Sundew *D. auriculata* with shield-shaped leaves and very long tentacles

could be added to the end, with an internal door leading into it from the warmhouse. Should there be exposure to cooling wind from any quarter, try to site the range so that the coolhouse, rather than the stovehouse or warmhouse, receives the brunt of it. Here is a summary of the temperature requirements of the various houses, together with some other information.

The coolhouse Accommodates the majority of cultivated species. In winter allow minimum night temperature of 4.5°C (40°F), but as warmer day temperatures are advisable try to ensure that the temperature does not fall below 10°C (50°F) during cold weather in the daylight hours. In summer a night minimum of 8°C (47°F) should be maintained, though in practice there is little risk of its ever falling below this at that time, particularly if you have automatic ventilation. Providing the tray system of watering is used, summer humidity should be adequate at most times, but in exceptionally hot weather it should be raised by damping down the greenhouse well with water once or twice a day. Apply light shading to the glass in late spring. Ventilate when the temperature rises above 20°C (68°F) in summer, and above 4.5°C (40°F) in winter. But consider issues of ventilation if gas or oil heaters are used.

The warmhouse Useful for growing some tropical species, and many sub-tropicals. Those sub-tropicals which can also be grown in the coolhouse will grow better here. Much cheaper to heat than a stovehouse, but only a limited range of tropicals will tolerate the lower temperature. It provides ideal conditions for Central American butterworts, epiphytic bladderworts and *Heliamphora* species. The remarks on humidity and shading for the coolhouse apply here also. In winter the night minimum should not fall below 13°C (55°F), and you should try to keep it above 15.5°C (60°F) by day. In summer, heating will not be necessary in warmer weather but will often be needed at night and sometimes in the daytime in cooler climates, allowing a summer night minimum of 18°C (65°F) and a day minimum of 21°C (70°F). Apply light shading to the glass in late spring. Ventilate when the temperature rises above 22°C (72°F) in summer, and above 15.5°C (60°F) in winter, and if gas or oil heaters are used see remarks above regarding the need for permanent ventilation in this case.

The stovehouse This reproduces the conditions of the tropical rainforest. In its high temperatures and dripping, highly humid atmosphere the fascinating lowland *Nepenthes* and their hybrids luxuriate, and you may also grow tropical bladderworts (see the *Nepenthes* chapter, pages 122–123).

The coldhouse Normally unheated, but it is wise to apply some heating during periods of freezing weather sufficiently to raise it just above freezing point, and in this way you will greatly increase the range of plants you can grow. Without this occasional heating the range is largely restricted to *Darlingtonia*, *Sarracenia flava*, *S. purpurea purpurea*, *S. oreophila*, *S. rubra jonesii*, the hybrids between these hardy species, and a few of the hardier sundews, *Pinguicula corsica* and *P. grandiflora* forms. With it you may additionally grow all the other *Sarracenia* species and all their hybrids, and the range of sundews may be broadened to include all North American species, *Drosera binata* 'T form', *Pinguicula vallisneriifolia*, and the Venus Fly Trap.

When you are heating, ventilation will need to be restricted, but at all other times every ventilator should be fully open except during high winds, while in summer the doors should also remain open. Apply shading in late spring. Humidity and damping down in the coolhouse apply equally in the coldhouse.

Heating Economic considerations may well have some influence on your decision as to the heating system you adopt. Fuel costs vary from year to year, from country to country, and there are pros and cons of alternative systems.

The coldframe The hardier hibernaculum-forming butterworts, with the exception of *Pinguicula vallisneriifolia*, are best grown in special coldframes. Structurally these are of the conventional kind, and the cheaper 'Dutch Light' sort is satisfactory. The tray system of watering means they must be level. The frame should be situated in a light place, but shaded from direct sunlight during the greater part of the day, especially in the hot midday period, or for the entire day. If this needs to be devised a tall panel of solid fence on its sunward side should suffice. The frame itself should face away from the sun. In winter keep the glass lights on the frame to protect the resting buds from the weather, which inevitably disturb and largely scatter the minute bud-like gemmae, though the frame should be kept well ventilated. In late spring or early summer remove these lights and replace with netting, to protect the pots from birds.

Few other carnivorous plants are suitable for such a shaded frame, but one exception is *Utricularia monanthos*, and some of the terrestrial bladderworts of North America. The sun-loving hardy sundews are also most easily grown in a frame. Follow the advice above in every way except let the frame be exposed to sun. No shading panel is needed and the frame can face the sunward side.

Arranging your plants A plant is only fully appreciated when it is displayed to best effect, and it is worth every effort to do this well. As a collection grows in size it all too easily degenerates into a higgledy-piggledy muddle and this is less often a reflection on any naturally untidy or disorganized habit of the owner than an unfortunate choice of containers and poor arrangement.

Colours Choose pots and containers of one colour, and wherever possible of one shape – square or round. The choice is yours, but bright colours can draw the eye from these plants. Your pots will have to be of different sizes to suit different plants, but try not to mix these, and wherever possible avoid mixing plants of radically different growth forms and dimensions, unless done deliberately for contrast. If you have the space your plants will look best if each container is placed a constant small distance away from its neighbours on each side.

Most plants are seen at their best if displayed at waist level on staging. Tiny species such as the pygmy sundews can be better appreciated nearer eye level on a shelf a little below the greenhouse eaves, while extra tall plants, such as

Sarracenia, Drosera and *Pinguicula* species out of doors in an artificial peat bog

Sarracenia flava 'Maxima', are best grown at floor level in all but the largest houses. They may be placed at the far end of the house or on one side of it where there is no staging.

In the largest collections, where space allows, a tableau landscaped in imitation of a natural bog shows off suitable plants well and can be a fascinating feature if carefully planned. To do so effectively you need a large quantity of material, and this can be an expensive venture if you have not propagated this from your own plants. The diagrams show the construction and a suggested planting scheme for such a tableau. The proportions can, of course, be varied, but too small a rectangle is not very effective. Plants suitable for inclusion are all *Sarracenia* species and hybrids, *Darlingtonia, Cephalotus, Drosera capensis, D. aliciae, D. spatulata* and all Fork-Leaved Sundews, *Pinguicula moranensis caudata*, terrestrial *Utricularia* species, Venus Fly Trap, and in the pond a medium-sized *Utricularia* such as *U. fibrosa*. Large quantities of *Drosera* species are easily produced for the

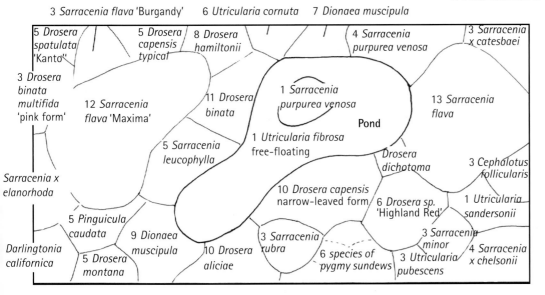

3 *Sarracenia flava* 'Burgandy'   6 *Utricularia cornuta*   7 *Dionaea muscipula*

5 *Drosera spatulata* 'Kanto'

5 *Drosera capensis typical*

8 *Drosera hamiltonii*

4 *Sarracenia purpurea venosa*

3 *Sarracenia x catesbaei*

3 *Drosera binata multifida* 'pink form'

12 *Sarracenia flava* 'Maxima'

11 *Drosera binata*

1 *Sarracenia purpurea venosa*

Pond

13 *Sarracenia flava*

5 *Sarracenia leucophylla*

1 *Utricularia fibrosa* free-floating

Drosera dichotoma

3 *Cephalotus follicularis*

Sarracenia x elanorhoda

10 *Drosera capensis* narrow-leaved form

6 *Drosera sp.* 'Highland Red'

1 *Utricularia sandersonii*

5 *Pinguicula caudata*

9 *Dionaea muscipula*

3 *Sarracenia rubra*

3 *Sarracenia minor*

Darlingtonia californica

5 *Drosera montana*

10 *Drosera aliciae*

6 species of pygmy sundews

3 *Utricularia pubescens*

4 *Sarracenia x chelsonii*

groups within months if raised from root and leaf cuttings.

CULTIVATION OUT OF DOORS

A large number of carnivorous plants can be grown out of doors if you live in a warm frost-free climate. But although the number of suitable species is reduced in cooler climates, such as Britain, some will respond well, while natives can be made to thrive as if in the wild. The plants can be made part of an attractive feature in the garden layout. There are three basic practical methods which are the Canal, Artificial Bog and Island Bog. In all cases the site should be sunny but protected from high winds, and you should avoid, at all costs, places adjoining sun-baked paving or walling. Evaporation will be high, so make sure you have an easily available supply of soft water.

The canal method In all its essentials this is the same as the tray system used in the greenhouse, except that the tray is in this case out of doors on the ground. The canal can be constructed using a liner of heavy-gauge black polythene sheet in almost the same way, the sides being supported with bricks or by timber. It can be of any length, the width being limited by how far you can conveniently stretch from both sides when tending your plants. Its base must be level, and this can be achieved by cultivating the surface to a fine tilth, raking this level, consolidating with the heels, raking it level again, consolidating again, and raking it level again. None of these operations must be done in wet weather.

Now take a board about 2.4m (7ft10in) long with perfectly straight and parallel sides, and use this to screed the surface. To do this place it on edge, hold a spirit-level on it, and keep it perfectly level so the loose soil can be spread until a near-perfect level is achieved. While doing this, crouch or kneel on a wide board

A suggested planting scheme for a tableau bog. All the *Drosera, Utricularia, Pinguicula* species and *Dionaea*, are easily propagated to the required quantities using the methods described in the text

PESTS AND DISEASES

These are dealt with under each section of the book, as they vary from genus to genus, and with conditions of cultivation.

Bog island in a pond.

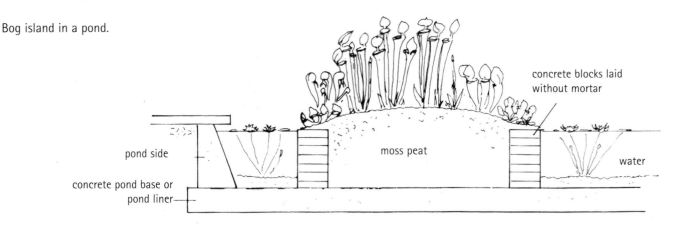

concrete blocks laid
without mortar

pond side

concrete pond base or
pond liner

moss peat

water

Drosera intermedia

to protect the surface. The sides of the canal, of loose bricks or rot-proofed timber secured with pegs, can now be placed in position. Pour enough shallow water in to keep it in place. The pots or containers may now be put in position. Always leave a space between the edges and the nearest pots, to foil slugs and snails. Always keep at least 2.5cm (1in) of water in the canal.

The artificial bog This is an exciting feature in the garden, and complements a rock or water garden. It is constructed like an artificial pond, but filled with moss peat instead of water. The immediate surrounds should be level, and, in limey soils in particular, not exposed to run-off from surrounding ground. It will not make much of an impact unless it's 1.20 x 1.20m (4 x 4ft). Excavate to a depth of 30–40cm (12–16in). See that the bottom is flat and that there are no sharp protruding objects, and cover it with about 13mm (0.5in) of builder's sand free of stone.

Now place the liner over the excavation, anchoring the sides with bricks or other heavy objects, but keeping the liner not quite taut. Pour sufficient lime-free water into it to weigh it down heavily, and gradually let the liner down into the excavation by lifting and replacing the weights around it until it touches the bottom over the whole area. Add enough water so that it forms a good fit after more lifting and replacement of the weights. Fill the structure with moist moss peat (sedge peat is not suitable), firming well as you progress. This will absorb the water in the bottom of the liner. When filled to within 2.5cm (1in) of the top, water well until the peat is saturated. It is important not to allow the peat along the edges to come into contact with the surrounding ground, for this will cause water to be sucked out of the bog, especially during dry spells (when soft water may be difficult to obtain), but the sides can be concealed by planting or paving. Ways of concealing the overlap of the liner are shown in the diagram above.

In the case of larger bogs it is a good plan to run a water ditch within the circumference of the sides, as this will prevent slugs, snails and other creeping or crawling pests entering the bog. Vary the contours within to suit various plants,

Bog pocket in a pond.

concrete blocks laid
without mortar

moss
peat

water

and have one or two shallow ponds for *Utricularia* in larger areas, while *Sarracenia purpurea purpurea* will appreciate really low-lying wet places that may become puddles during rainy periods.

Birds often like to root about in the wet peat in search of grubs – least disturbed will be groups of robust growers, such as the *Sarracenias*, rather than little ones. Small growers such as hardy sundews can then be introduced later among the protective bulk of the pitcher plants. Never introduce sphagnum – this is an invitation to every bird to come on missions of pure vandalism!

The island bog A major source of interest in any garden, and it can be constructed in almost any pond in which the water is lime-free. Since it is isolated from the land, there is little risk of slugs and snails gaining a foothold, unless you include a bridge from the 'mainland' or have a continuous sheet of water-lily pads between. It is best placed near that side of the pond where you are most often likely to be, to appreciate the fine details of its planting, and within stepping distance when weeding becomes necessary.

Construction is simple. The sides of the island may be built with concrete blocks laid dry without mortar. Clearly, if your pond is constructed with a liner the weight might rupture this, and in this case lay that area of the liner over concrete slabs set perfectly level, and ensure that the blocks have no sharp projections where they are in contact with the liner. If the pond is not more than about 30cm (1ft) deep, there should be no need for the slab foundation. The top course, which is to project above the water, is best constructed of real stone to give a natural effect, but this must not be of limestone. Then fill the enclosed area with moist moss peat (not sedge peat) and consolidate well with your feet. Make humps in the island here and there to make it appear natural, and one or two judiciously placed rocks will help to give the impression that the rocky shoreline is natural. The concrete blocks below water-level will at first appear anything but natural, but will soon become covered with algae and other vegetation, and may be masked even before this with suitable aquatic planting. Bog pockets at the side of ponds can be constructed in much the same manner, and although these can provide magnificent sites for hardy *Sarracenias* it is difficult to prevent slugs and snails consuming the young pitcher growth of these plants.

Planting the bog If you live in a warm, frost-free climate almost everything suitable for the cool greenhouse may also be grown in the artificial bog, the obvious exceptions being those plants that require special conditions, such as *Drosophyllum* and the tuberous sundews. In cooler places subject to winter frosts the range that will succeed is much more limited. As the severity of such climates varies, trial and error is often the only way to establish what will succeed in a particular spot, but even where winters are quite harsh you may expect the following selection to thrive: *Sarracenia purpurea purpurea*, *Pinguicula vulgaris*, *Drosera anglica*, *DD. rotundifolia, intermedia, x obovata, x beleziana* and *linearis*, and *Darlingtonia californica*. These can survive a temperature of -11°C (12°F) in winter. In addition to the above species the following have proved hardy: *Sarracenia flava* forms, *SS. oreophila, rubra* ssp. *rubra, rubra* ssp. *jonesii, x catesbaei, x melanorhoda, x popei*. Other hybrids with any of these plants as parents are likely to be hardy, as are *Drosera filiformis* var. *filiformis*, *Pinguicula grandiflora* forms and its subspecies *rosea*, and *P. lusitanica*. Try *Utricularia monanthos*, which has already proved hardy in a coldframe, and all North American terrestrial *Utricularias*. Where water is included in the bog, the hardy *Utricularias* native to your own area are available, of course, and *UU. intermedia* and *minor* are good candidates for shallow water in Europe and North America. *Drosera binata* can survive in a peat bog for many years. A Venus Fly Trap will survive only mild winters, so protect with a glass cloche and a temporary straw covering in winter.

To give the bog a more natural look, include a few non-carnivorous natives of peat bogs, if they are non-invasive or easily controlled, such as Grass of Parnassus *Parnassia palustris*, Cranberry *Vaccinium oxycoccus*, Bog Pimpernel *Anagallis tenella*, Bog Asphodel *Narthecium ossifragum*, Bog Rosemary *Andromeda polifolia*, and from the North American savannahs the White Bracted Sedge *Dichromena latifolia*, Hatpins *Eriocaulon compressum*, and Yellow-Eyed Grass *Xyris torta*.

The Sundews: Drosera

Not only does it catch and digest its prey with great efficiency, but the sundew possesses all the qualities essential to the popular image of the carnivorous plant. Most of the species are distinctly beautiful in leaf and often in flower and are worth cultivating for these reasons alone. There are now about 100 recognized species, from many parts of the world. Although their leaves occur in a wide variety of shapes and sizes, all possess tentacles on the upper surface and margin of each leaf. These tentacles are usually pinkish to red, each terminating in a roundish, often red, gland-bearing a dew-like droop of fluid. Sticky, colourless and crystal-clear, the numerous drops sparkle in the light like diamonds, giving an

The Paddle-leaved Sundew *(Drosera x obovata)* is a natural hybrid between *D. rotundifolia* and *D. Angelica.* It can be larger than the latter and inherits much of its character

Drosera sp. 'Bannister'

almost ethereal quality to the foliage. Alighting insects stick to this 'glue', and through their struggles to escape stimulate surrounding tentacles into action, so that they bend over and hold the victim. Swamped with their mucilage, it is soon suffocated. At this stage the same glands start to secrete another fluid which digests the soft parts of its body, making a highly nutritious liquid which is then absorbed into the plant's system by the glands. In many species the leaf blade itself is capable of folding over its prey. This usually happens when the creature is already dead, and by this means more glandular leaf surface is brought into contact with the prey, allowing more efficient digestion.

EASY GROWERS

From a confusingly wide range of available species, where can a beginner start? For the window-sill, *D. aliciae*, followed by the other species mentioned on page 9. In the coolhouse *D. capensis* narrow-leaved form, followed by *DD. binata multifida* Pink Form, *aliciae*, sp. 'Bannister', *regia* sp. 'Highland Red', and *occidentalis*, in that order. All these are easy growers which display a wide variety of foliage, flower and colour.

General cultivation Unless stated otherwise, all the species described in this chapter will succeed in the coolhouse and can be very easily cultivated as follows. Plant firmly in a well-mixed compost of 1 part horticultural sand to 3 parts granulated moss peat. Do not use a smaller size of pot than that recommended. Irrigate by the tray system, using soft water. Your plants must be in a sunny position, though light shading should be applied in late spring and removed in early autumn.

   Propagation Different methods suit different species. Here are the three basic ones, the fourth (division) is rarely used.

   Seed is best sown in spring. The exceptions are the winter growers, where seed should be sown in autumn. Use standard *Drosera* compost in plastic seed boxes or shallow dwarf pots. Firm the surface with a flat object so that it is level, and scatter the seed sparsely. Do not bury it or use any cover, and stand it permanently in the water tray in a sunny position. Germination usually occurs in six to eight weeks' time, but some tuberous species (e.g. *D. erythrorhiza*) may take two years or even longer. When large enough to handle, dig them up carefully so as not to injure the root systems. They may either be potted directly, or temporarily pricked out about 4cm (1.5in) apart in seed boxes.

   Leaf cuttings Mature plants of some species can be produced within months: take cuttings between late spring and high summer. Just fill a plastic seed box with standard *Drosera* compost to within 6mm (0.25in) of the brim, firming this with a flat object so that it is level. Take some live green sphagnum moss (no other moss will do), squeeze the water out of it and repeatedly break with the fingers until it is very fine. Now scatter this over the surface of the compost, gently spreading it so as to form the thinnest continuous layer; press it so that it is as smooth as possible, and lightly wet it with soft water, using the fine sprinkler on your can.

Now select healthy, mature leaves on your plant (i.e. fully open leaves secreting from all their tentacles). The cuts should be made with a really sharp knife or razor. In most cases make the cut as near to the base of the leaf-stalk as possible, and use the whole leaf. In *D. filiformis* the leaf is best cut into short lengths 12–25mm (0.5–1in) long, while in *D. binata* and its varieties the blade can be conveniently divided into two or several pieces.

Lay the cuttings flat on the sphagnum bed, top side uppermost, and so that one cutting does not quite touch another, and just cover from view with the thinnest layer of more finely broken live sphagnum. Again lightly water to settle this layer around the cuttings. The box should then be placed in the water tray in a sunny position in the greenhouse, except in the cases of the Queensland Sundews which should be placed in the same humid, shaded conditions as their parents. The young plants arise from adventitious buds, which form at the base of some of the tentacles, and several may be formed on one leaf. They arise at often irregular intervals from six weeks to several months after taking the cuttings.

Root cuttings can be used for some species which form thick fleshy roots, such as the *D. binata* varieties and *D. regia*. Take a well-established, vigorous plant, tap it out of its pot, and providing a good root system is in evidence you can remove one of the larger exposed roots without any ill effects for the plant. Cut this root cleanly with a razor or sharp knife into lengths 12–25mm (0.5–1in) long. Fill a plastic seed box to within 6mm (0.25in) of its brim with standard sundew compost, firming with a flat object to make it level. The root cuttings are then spaced out flat upon the surface, so that they do not touch. Now cover with a 3mm (0.12in) layer of the compost, and stand in the water tray in a light position of the greenhouse. The first shoots are usually seen in six to ten weeks' time.

Attack from pests and diseases is rare. Occasionally greenfly may affect young undeveloped foliage and flowering stems, but are easily removed with a watercolour brush dipped in the sticky mucilage from the tentacles.

THE SPECIES

The numerous and varied species of Drosera is divided, for simplicity and convenience, into several categories based on their area of occurrence or their form of growth.

ROSETTE-FORMING SUNDEWS

Some of the most easily grown of all sundews are suitable for a sunny window-sill as well as for the greenhouse. All those listed will succeed in the coolhouse, tolerating a winter minimum of around 4.5°C (40°F), and are best watered on the tray system.

A large number of species arrange their leaves in flat rosettes. The Spoon-Leaf, or Spatulate Sundew *D. spatulata* are worth growing, and in catalogues are usually named after the geographical places to which they are native. Their leaves are usually, but not always, spatula-shaped, and the rosette reaches a maximum

Drosera villosa

diameter of 3.5cm (1.4in) in most forms. From Japan, 'Kanto' has intensely red wedge-shaped leaves, and flower stalks to 20cm (8in) bearing many small pink flowers. 'Kansai' has similar flowers but leaves which are pinkish and spoon-shaped, while in 'Okinowa' the very pale pink flowers are larger and borne on longer flower stalks.

Rather smaller forms occur in Hong Kong, with rosy pink or white flowers. In the typical New Zealand form the leaf blade is round with a little red coloration, while the flowers are snow white, but there is also a pink form. There is also a rather large white-flowered form from Tanega Island. In Australia the flowers vary from white to rose, the leaves being always spoon-shaped. Plant singly in a 10cm (4in) pot, or several in a 12.5cm (5in) dwarf pot. Propagate by seed or leaf cuttings.

The Mountain Sundew *Drosera montana* is native to Venezuela and Brazil and needs the same treatment. It is quite similar to *D. spatulata* in foliage – wedge-shaped but rather narrower, bronze to greenish pink – but the typically white flowers are smaller. It was introduced to cultivation from Mount Roraima; its form var. *roraimae* has gradually forming long stems on which the solitary rosette is perched. Reaching this point in the process must take the plant many years.

Like a minute version of *D. spatulata*, the Short-Leafed Sundew *D. brevifolia* is common on the Gulf Coast of America. Its rosette of reddish wedge-shaped leaves seldom exceeds 2cm (?in) in diameter. A short-lived perennial, it regenerates satisfactorily from self-sown seed which, on *Drosera* compost in a 12.5cm (5in) dwarf pot, will result in a glittering carpet of reddish leaves surmounted by little flower stalks of pink to white flowers.

From the US, Central and South America, the Pink Sundew *D. capillaries* can easily be mistaken for the Round-Leaved Sundew *D. rotundifolia* in leaf, but it forms no resting bud in winter, and the leaf blade is longer than wide. The flowers are, however, larger, and can be pink or white. A large-leaved form occurs on the Gulf Coast, while a narrow-leaved form with foliage similar to that of *D. intermedia* has been introduced from a bog in Florida. All are short-lived perennials, but are easily raised from seed or leaf cuttings. Plant several to a 12.5cm (5in) dwarf pot.

Occurring in bogs in the extreme south-west of Western Australia, *D. hamiltonii* forms large flat rosettes up to 5cm (2in) across. The slim, somewhat succulent, wedge-shaped leaves turn an attractive brownish coral-pink when exposed to sunlight. But perhaps its chief claim to glory is its huge flowers, several of which are borne aloft on a tall, wiry, purplish stalk. They are of a lively lilac purple, cup-shaped and as much as 3.5cm (1.4in) in diameter. Constantly moving in even the slightest draught, from a distance they can be confused with hovering butterflies. Grow in a 12.5cm (5in) pot, and propagate from root or leaf cuttings.

THE DWARF FORM

In its typical form the rosette of the Brazilian *D. villosa* can become huge, often exceeding 11cm (4.3in) in diameter. This consists of arching, strap-shaped, pinkish-red leaves noticeably hairy on the undersides, narrowing to rounded ends. The flower stalks can reach 50cm (20in), often branching once or twice, and bear up to forty deep-rose yellow-stamened flowers. The dwarf form 'Orgelgeburge' has flat rosettes to 4cm (1.5in) across, and short flower stalks of up to twelve paler flowers. Use a 12.5cm (5in) dwarf pot for the first, but a 10cm (4in) pot will be adequate for the latter. Both may be propagated from seed.

Though at best a short-lived perennial, *D. burmanni* is of special interest on account of its extra-long outer tentacles. These are capable of very quick movement, often completing a bend of 180° in less than twenty seconds. The roundish blades are usually pale green, but may become suffused with purple in sunlight, and the rosette is up to 2.5cm (1in) in diameter, bearing long purplish stalks of up to twelve white flowers. This is a tropical to sub-tropical species, ranging from Japan to Australia, but it can do well in the coolhouse if grown from seed sown in mid-spring, dying in the autumn. It often survives for more than a

The large vivid rosettes of 'Highland Red'

Drosera sp. 'Highland Red' flowers

year under a light in a heated terrarium, and it would make a good subject for the warmhouse. A 12.5cm (5in) dwarf pot can accommodate several plants.

The Woolly Sundew *D. petiolaris* occurs in tropical parts of northern Australia, and must be grown in appropriately warm conditions, either in a greenhouse with a minimum temperature of 18.5°C (65°F) and shaded from direct sunlight, or in a heated terrarium, with these same conditions. Use a 12.5cm (5in) dwarf pot. It is a distinctive species. The leaves may reach 5cm (2in) in length, and comprise a long, flat, gradually broadening, somewhat glaucous stalk which abruptly narrows at the end to a tiny round blade up to 3mm (0.12in) across, with purple tentacles. The leaves rise from a base which often appears woolly due to finely divided and bristle-like stipules, and may form massive rosettes to as much as 10cm (4in) in diameter. The flower stalks are up to 25cm (10in) long, and bear many white or pink flowers.

SUNDEWS FROM SOUTH AFRICA

South Africa is renowned for the wealth and beauty of its flora, and certainly some of the most lovely sundews are natives of the area. Unless otherwise stated, all these described come from the Cape Province. Most are easy growers, and one which succeeds as a sunny window-sill plant and in the coolhouse is the Alice Sundew *D. aliciae*. Its flattish rosettes of wedge-shaped leaves may reach 5cm (2in) in diameter and are perfectly circular. The foliage is mid-green and decorated with vivid red tentacles. The scapes are up to 35cm (14in) long, and bear many soft lilac-pink flowers 1.3cm (0.5in) across, with conspicuous yellow stamens. It has a long root system, and should therefore be given a suitably large pot. You can accommodate seven in a 12.5cm (5in) pot, in a ring with one in the centre. Propagation is easy, from leaf cuttings or seed. There are a number of other very similar species which require identical treatment. Of these, *D. cuneifolia* has wedge-shaped, wider but much shorter leaves in rosettes to about 2.5cm (1in) in diameter, but the flowers are larger and of a more intense colour. In *D. natalensis* the rosette may be 5cm (2in) in diameter, but the leaves are narrower and distinctly spoon-shaped. The flowers may be pale to deep pink, and are a beautiful shade of flesh pink in the form generally favoured. *D. dielsiana* is an almost perfect copy of *D. aliciae* but about a third its size. Its flowers are quite large for so small a plant, and are a lovely soft rosy pink.

DISCOVERIES

A number of closely allied plants have been discovered and introduced relatively recently which differ botanically from other forms and need clarification. All are worth growing. Quite the most remarkable is one which was discovered by an amateur botanist, Mr Frank Woodvine. He was searching for a rare bog *Protea* in the Kleinrivierberge Mountains not far from the seaside resort of Hermanus in the south-west Cape Province. He was following a small brook to its source when suddenly he spotted a brilliant red blaze on the side of a bend in the stream. On

closer examination it turned out to be large colony of a sundew with brilliant-red foliage, which he took to be a form of *D. aliciae*. Here it grew in close company with such plants as *Drosera glabripes*, *Roridula gorgonias* and *Utricularia capensis*, at an elevation of between 500 and 700m in the moist cloud belt, never more than one mile from the sea. This is not only one of the most beautiful of all sundews, but also, horticulturally, its introduction is one of the most important amongst carnivorous plants in recent years. The leaf is noticeably different from that of *D. aliciae*, and a cultivated plant in Britain has reached 6.5cm (2.5in). The bronzy flower stems are thick, erect and wiry, and bear up to fifteen splendid flowers, reaching 27mm (1.06in) in diameter, much larger than in *D. aliciae*. The petals are heather-pink and of great substance, while the unusually wide, pure-white stamens with their yellow-orange pollen are a conspicuous feature. (These differ very much from those of *D. aliciae*, as do the styles, and I feel that this must be seen as a new species, which for convenience I have temporarily named *D. sp. 'Highland Red'*. Cultivate as for *D. aliciae*. Easily raised from leaf cuttings, root cuttings and seed.)

Growing in plains not far from this mountain, Mr Woodvine discovered another distinct sundew which became known as *D. sp. 'Plains Form'*, but though there are differences in the flower it is near enough to *D. aliciae* to be considered a form of that species. The leaf rosettes are slightly smaller than in the typical form of the *aliciae* and the flower is of an especially delicate shade of mauve-pink. Treat and propagate as for *D. aliciae*.

By no means do all South African sundews share the tight rosetted habit of those just described. Indeed, they show a very great diversity. One of the showiest is the Cape Sundew, *D. capensis*, and this always excites interest when its strap-

Left: A fly struggles to escape from the tentacles of the Cape Sundew *D. capensis*. A leaf blade completely encircles the body of an earlier visitor

Centre: *D. cistiflora*

Above: *D. cistiflora* in bloom. The Cistus-Flowered Sundew is notable for its gigantic flowers

Above: The King Sundew *D. regia* has the largest leaf blades of any species

Below: The leaf blade and tentacles of *D. rotundifolia* work together in the capture and digestion of a large victim

shaped leaves are seen enfolding its prey, often winding round its body two or more times. In the typical form the leaf blade measures up to about 3.8cm (1.5in) long x 8mm (0.31in) wide, of spring green with red contrasting tentacles, and the stalk is about the same length. The leaves are arranged in a loose rosette about 15cm (6in) in diameter. The plant gradually develops a stalk and in nature adopts a semi-trailing habit. The flowering stems may reach 35cm (14in) and bear many rosy pink flowers up to 2cm (0.78in) across. There is also the narrow-leaved form, which scarcely forms a stem at all, and is rather smaller and neater in growth. Its foliage is narrower, the flowers rather smaller, and it flowers earlier. You will find that each is sufficiently distinct and attractive to justify growing both forms. Plant both in 12.5cm (5in) dwarf pots and propagate from leaf cuttings or seed.

The Hilarious Sundew *D. hilaris* is rather like a larger edition of the typical form of *D. capensis*, except that the leaf blade is narrowly oval rather than strap-shaped, and of paler green. These leaves bend and straggle about in every direction, giving the plant a clownish, intoxicated air which explains its Latin and English names. The flowers, too, are similar, but it differs in having a summer resting period, at which stage the compost should be kept moist rather than wet. Plant in a 12.5cm (5in) full-length or larger pot, for it has long succulent roots which need room. Do not disturb it during dormancy. When growth recommences, transfer again to the water tray. Propagate from seed sown in late summer or early autumn, or from leaf cuttings.

NO ESCAPE

Rare in nature, of unique habit and a giant, is the King Sundew *D. regia*, yet it is simple enough to grow. The leaves are rolled in the bud, uncoiling to a length of up to 46cm (18in) in fully mature plants, though it is slow to reach that size. They are sword-shaped, tapering to a narrow point, erect to arching, of mid-green with dark red tentacles. The flowers are pink to purple, and up to 3.5cm (1.4in) across. These are borne in a cluster on a stem barely longer than the leaves. Unlike many Narrow-Leaved Sundews the leaves will bend over their prey, and this can lead to quaintly knotted leaves when several victims have been caught on the same blade. The minimum pot size should be 12.5cm (5in). The plants have a short period of semi-dormancy in winter when very small modified leaves are produced, but sometimes the entire crown will die, and if this happens the plant must not be discarded or disturbed for it will almost certainly shoot again from the roots in spring. Keep in the water tray at all times. Propagate from root cuttings, for in my experience leaf cuttings never succeed. Seed will germinate, but seedlings may take up to three years to reach maturity.

Drosera glabripes is a newcomer to cultivation and almost shrub-like in growth. The stems are narrow and occasionally dividing, and may grow to a length of several feet in nature. They bear leaves that are up to 3cm (1.2in) long, green with red tentacles and narrowly spatula-shaped. The flowers are said to be small and pink but it is a shy flowerer. Grow in 12.5cm (5in) pots. Propagate from seed.

The rare Long-Stemmed Sundew *D. ramentacea*, with purple flowers, is very similar and presumably will need the same treatment. Also *D. madagascariensis*, a native of Madagascar as well as South Africa, may need warmhouse conditions.

Another large grower, the Cistus-Flowered Sundew *D. cistiflora* is also one of the most lovely. It is a winter grower, dying back by early summer. It produces a leafy stem to about 30cm (1ft) which may branch once to several times. The leaves vary in width, but are usually narrow, up to 10cm (4in) long, bright green with red tentacles. The cup-shaped flowers, up to 7.5cm (3in), are the largest in the entire genus, and may be white, pale to deep rose, mauve, and in one splendid form, brilliant scarlet, one to several being borne to a stalk. Grow in a 15cm (6in) pot. It is good to keep the compost moist even during its long resting period. Propagation is best by leaf cuttings. Seed can also be sown, but they will take several years to form good plants.

Drosera collinsiae is a small plant with foliage similar to *D. intermedia*, except that the leaves are bright green. The flowers are a pretty rose pink, with several to a stalk. It has been thought to be of hybrid origin – possibly *D. burkeana x D. madagascariensis* – but this is doubtful for one of my plants produced a little seed one year, and no other hybrid *Drosera* I know of has done this. A 10cm (4in) pot is large enough, and you may raise it from leaf cuttings. *D. trinerva* has narrowly wedge-shaped leaves forming flat rosettes to 2.5cm (1in) wide. The scapes are up to 7cm (2.75in) high and bear several white flowers. It has a period of summer dormancy. *D. burkei* is a small grower and like a tiny *D. spatulata*, a form of which has too often been paraded under this name in cultivation. The wedge-shaped leaves are typically brownish-pink, and the small flowers are usually white. Treat as for *D. spatulata*.

SOME HARDY SUNDEWS

In cooler parts of the northern hemisphere the majority of sundews die down to a 'resting bud' in winter, properly called a hibernaculum (plural: hibernacula). This includes all those native to Europe and the majority of North American species. The best known representative of this group is no doubt the Round-Leaved Sundew *D. rotundifolia*, a pretty plant widely distributed in the peat bogs of moors and mountains in North America, Europe, Russia and Asia. The leaves are more or less circular, on long stalks rising from a flat rosette to about 5cm (2in) diameter. They are often red-tinted, and have red gland-tipped tentacles. The narrow flower stalk bears several small white flowers which open around midday on sunny days.

This plant prefers to grow on living sphagnum moss, and the mere presence of this moss in a locality means that the sundew is almost certainly present. Like all other members of this group, this plant should be grown outside in the open frame or artificial bog, or you may try it in a well-ventilated coldhouse. It can be grown in colonies in a 12.5cm (5in) dwarf pot, and allowed to seed itself in this. The best potting medium is pure live sphagnum moss, but if this is difficult to obtain it will also grow in standard *Drosera* compost. It is easily propagated from seed; also from leaf cuttings, which should be raised in the coolhouse around mid-summer, and not placed in the coldframe until they are shooting.

The Great or English Sundew *D. anglica* occurs in North America, Europe and Japan. It is rare in England despite its Latin name, though common in the Western Highlands of Scotland and in Ireland. The leaf often exceeds 7.5cm (3in) in length, is oar-shaped with a rounded top, the blade merging so gradually with the stem that it is difficult to tell where one or the other begins or ends. It is olive-green with red tentacles. The flower stalk arises from the centre of the plant and bears several white flowers, considerably larger than those of *D. rotundifolia*. It requires the same treatment.

The Love Nest Sundew *D. intermedia* is sometimes mistaken for *D. anglica*, but is (in the typical form) half its size. There is also a distinct division between leaf stem and blade, and the flower stems rise from the side rather than the centre of the rosette, bearing much smaller flowers. It is usually found growing on very wet, naked peat, often in shallow seeping water. Plant in pure peat in shallow containers so as to keep the water table high. Again, it is a subject for the coldframe or bog. A fine giant form over twice the size is found growing in parts of the south-eastern United States.

The Paddle-Leaved Sundew *D. x obovata* is the natural hybrid between *D. rotundifolia* and *D. anglica*, and can even surpass the English Sundew in size and magnificence, the chief difference being that the upright leaf is shaped like an old-fashioned canoe paddle. *D. x beleziana* is the natural hybrid between *D. rotundifolia* and *D. intermedia*, and looks somewhat like a Round-Leaved Sundew, except that the leaves are oval and the foliage is borne at all angles from upright to semi-prostrate in a humped rosette. Growing the form in which the *D. intermedia* parent is the giant American type mentioned above, has resulted in an extra large hybrid up to 7.5cm (3in) in diameter, and one of the most attractive. These hybrids cannot be grown from seed, but come well from leaf cuttings. Otherwise treat as for *D. rotundifolia*.

The Linear Sundew *D. linearis*, from the American Great Lakes region, differs from all other species in favouring alkaline conditions in marl bogs. The leaves are erect, up to 4cm (1.5in) long, while the blade is almost as narrow as the stalk, bearing red tentacles. Several small white flowers are borne to the scape. Treat as for *D. intermedia* (in practice, the acidity does not hurt it) and propagate from seed.

Hibernacula-forming, too, but of very different appearance, are the Thread-Leaved Sundews of the US. There are two sub-species. *D. filiformis* ssp. *filiformis* occurs principally in New Jersey and bears upright, thread-like green leaves up to 24cm (9.4in) long, bearing red glands. The erect wiry scapes bear many deep rose flowers to about 15mm (0.6in) in diameter. Larger altogether, *D. filiformis* ssp. *tracyi* has leaves to 5cm (2in), in which the tentacles entirely lack red coloration. Erect in the wild, they are semi-erect to spreading in cultivation. The flowers are of paler rose and larger, 2cm (0.78in) across. A southerner, it occurs in Georgia, northern Florida and the Gulf Coast. A beautiful hybrid between the two is, *D. x*

'California Sunset', with large flowers of rose pink and large foliage with reddish glands, which has a neater, less spreading habit than cultivated ssp. *tracyi*. I prefer to grow all these three in ordinary *Drosera* compost in 12.5cm (5in) pots in the coldframe, in cold winters or climates colder than Britain, ssp. *tracyi* and 'California Sunset' can succumb to frost attack, so should be overwintered in a frost-proofed coldhouse or a coolhouse. Alternatively, you may overwinter juvenile resting buds raised from leaf cuttings by washing them and placing them, sealed in a plastic bag, in the main compartment of the refrigerator. Propagation can be from seed, except in the case of the hybrid, but much the best method is from leaf cuttings. A natural hybrid between *D. filiformis* ssp. *filiformis* and *D. intermedia* occurs in New Jersey. This, *D. x hybrida*, is clump-forming and the leaves are like a rather shorter version of ssp. *filiformis*, except that they inherit the mobility of *D. intermedia*. The small flowers are very pale pink. Best treated as for *D. rotundifolia*, and very effective when grown in colonies in the bog. Propagate from division and leaf cuttings. A vigorous and most attractive plant.

The following two species die down for the winter but do not form true hibernacula. *D. arcturi* is an alpine plant from the mountains of New Zealand and Australia. It has several strap-shaped leaves up to 10cm (4in) long, and a short flower stalk bearing a solitary white flower up to 16mm (0.62in) across. Grow in standard *Drosera* compost in a 12.5cm (5in) dwarf pot, propagating it from seed. The Wahu Sundew *D. stenopetala* from New Zealand is rather smaller, with strap-like leaves to 7cm (2.75in) long, and white flowers. It grows from lowland levels to alpine heights above 1500m, so is assumed to be reasonably hardy and will respond to the same treatment.

THE FORK-LEAVED SUNDEWS

Sundews in this group all have forked foliage, and include some of the largest-leaved of all species. All are natives of the eastern coast of Australia, and one variety occurs in New Zealand also.

The foliage arises from the base and consists of a long, rather flat-leaf stalk which supports a long, narrow blade which immediately forks once, and in most forms two or more times. The outer tentacles of the blade are unusually long, and each final division of the blade narrows to a point which is crowned with a crest-like cluster of even longer, though immobile, ones. The large flowers are white, or occasionally pink, and are borne on long racemes which may fork into two or three branches.

Although the following plants are all considered to be variants of one species, *D. binata*, they differ very much in leaf and flower. All are for the coolhouse and standard *Drosera* compost. Propagation can be by root cuttings, leaf cuttings or division. Seed can result in inferior clones.

D. binata 'T Form' has been in cultivation in Europe for well over a century. The blades fork only once, the entire leaf being about 30cm (12in) tall. The blade is olive-green, often suffused with red, and the tentacles intensely red, so that a

The Staghorn Sundew *D. binata* var. *dichotoma* in flower

clump of the plant appears deep red from a distance, with contrasting snow-white flowers. To grow as a group in a seed box or in a similar container, space the root cuttings about 4cm (1.5in) apart. Otherwise use a 12.5cm (5in) dwarf pot.

In the typical form of *D. binata* var. *multifida*, the leaves closely resemble those of the above, except that in the mature plant they commonly fork to produce six to eight final divisions or 'points'. The petals are narrower, however, and unless subjected to excessive cold the plant does not become completely dormant in winter. Treat as 'T Form'.

A splendid giant var. *multifida* 'Extrema', can reach up to 90cm (3ft) in height in its native Stradbroke Island near Brisbane, when growing amongst reed. In cultivation, its pendant leaves are seldom much more than 30cm (1ft) long, but the blades can divide repeatedly to form well over 40 points on some, and are tinted a rich crimson in sunlight. It is seen best as a hanging-basket plant, or as a specimen piece in a 30cm (12in) pot, both giving the leaves space to hang. The flowers are wide petalled and of good substance, but they look out of keeping with its weeping habit and the flower stalks are best removed. Again, it does not normally become completely dormant. There is also a beautiful pink form of var. *multifida*, the flowers being quite substantial and of a particularly lovely pearly rose. This has a short dormant period in winter. Treat and propagate as for the typical form.

In the largest and generally cultivated form of the Staghorn Sundew *D. binata* var. *dichotoma* leaves can reach 58cm (23in) in length. It is easily distinguished from other varieties by its yellowy-green blades, which are noticeably wide and branch less regularly, so that you may find leaves with anything from two to eight points on a mature plant. The tentacles are of the same colour, but are crowned with red glands. The flower stalks are up to 76cm (30in) in height, bearing the largest flowers in this group – about 2.5cm (1in) in diameter. There is a brief winter dormancy. Grow this in a 15cm (6in) pot, otherwise cultivating and propagating as for *D. binata* 'T Form'. There is a fine smaller var. *dichotoma* 'T Form' which has smaller leaves which fork only once, like the other 'T Form', with which it makes a fine colour contrast. In every other way it resembles and behaves like the typical var. *dichotoma*, and its flowers are as large. Cultivate and propagate as for that variety.

'MARSTON DRAGON'

Hybrid seedlings between the varieties are seldom satisfactory, and I was fortunate in selecting one solitary seedling in 1983 which has proved itself to be of exceptional quality, and which I have named *D. binata x* 'Marston Dragon'. Its pendulous stems are up to 36cm (14in) long and bear blades the segments of which are as wide as those of *dichotoma*, and are the largest I have seen in this section. They divide irregularly into two to eight points and are the same yellowish green as in *D. dichotoma*, but the reddish-pink tentacles render them more attractive. A curious characteristic of the blade is the manner in which the segments spread sideways, often to a great length, the points curving round and clutching the air like talons, the whole reminding one very much of the feet of a Chinese dragon. The flowers are large and are borne on long straight scapes, but hardly seem to suit the weeping habit, especially if the plant is in a hanging basket, so it best to remove them. In every respect give the same treatment as for *D. multifida* 'Extrema'.

SUNDEWS OF THE NORTH QUEENSLAND RAINFORESTS

There are three sundews which differ from all the others mentioned due to their hatred of direct sunlight, which will burn their foliage and eventually kill the plant. This makes them an excellent choice for sunless windows. Coming from tropical rainforest, they also require high humidity, but this is easily provided if the pot is covered with a propagating dome, a bell-glass, or placed in a terrarium, especially if it is heated (see page 12). Normal coolhouse temperatures are a little cold for them unless you live in a suitably warm climate, but they make good warmhouse subjects. In this case they must both be covered with a propagating cover and be shaded from direct sun. The winter minimum should not sink below 10°C (50°F). Water on the tray system.

A rarity from Mount Bartle Frere, the Notched Sundew *D. schizandra* is a magnificent species which is all too often seen as a sickly dwarf, due to too frequent division. It is one of those plants which must be left undisturbed to prosper, and will reward you by growing larger and more splendid foliage and flowers annually over a period of several years. The plants are clump-forming and need room, so start in 10cm (4in) pots, using standard *Drosera* compost and transfer to 12.5cm (5in) dwarf pot the following year. When these become filled by daughter rosettes in three to four years' time, you may either divide or transfer to a larger dwarf pot. Propagate by leaf cuttings. Division can be used, too, but this retards development of the parent. In a well-developed plant the leaves can reach 10cm (4in) in length. They are wedge-shaped, of lettuce green with sparsely scattered red glands. In larger plants their rounded ends often become notched distinctively at the centre. In the best cultivated form the flowers, too, are very splendid. They are borne in a cluster on short flower stalks, sometimes with several being open at one time. They are up to 1cm (0.4in) in diameter, of a pinkish red.

Although the Lance-Leaved Sundew *D. adelae* is closely related to the *D. schizandra*, it looks quite different. The sword-shaped foliage is up to 7.5cm (3in) in cultivation, green to bronzy-red with dark red tentacles. The numerous flowers are star-shaped and borne on tall stalks. In the long-cultivated form they are biscuit-coloured and somewhat dull, but in the red-flowered form they are most attractive, the yellow stamens setting off the rich dark red of the petals well. Use a 12.5cm (5in) pot, otherwise cultivate and propagate as for *D. schizandra*. Often the occasional rosette of an established plant will die. Do not throw the plant away, but simply clip it off just below the rosette at ground level, and almost invariably it will be replaced by sucker growth in a few weeks' time.

The Rusty Sundew *D. dichrosepala*. Its large white flowers are above the delicate, sparkling rosettes. Note the silvery-white stipules

The Hen and Chickens Sundew *D. prolifera* is a close cousin of both the above, yet again differs in appearance from them. The leaves are long-stalked, somewhat like those of the Round-Leaved Sundew but larger, gradually ascending, with kidney-shaped blades. The latter are lettuce green and red-glanded.

The long flower stalk is unusual in being borne sideways, almost horizontally, so that the tip touches the ground. It bears two to several, widely separated, small red flowers along its length. A bud develops at the end that touches the ground, and this produces leaves and roots, forming a new plant. In this way the plant can form large colonies, and also produce viable seed. Grow and propagate as recommended for *D. schizandra*, but it is preferable to plant in a wider dwarf pot or shallow container to allow room for proliferation.

THE PYGMY SUNDEWS
All these species are of Australasian origin, the vast majority being natives of Western Australia and are some of the most fascinating as well as some of the most beautiful and collectable of all sundews. On the one hand you will find delightful miniatures and, on the other, plants remarkable for the beauty of their flowers, which individually may exceed the diameter of the leaf rosette itself. They occur in a vast range of hue and colour, from pale pink to peach through orange to brightest vermilion, and from creamy white to vivid chrome yellow, while many are bicolours. But if your interest is in traps alone you will not be disappointed. Even the tiniest are highly efficient, although their food may include nothing

much larger than a springtail, while some – *D. dichrosepala*, for instance – have some extra-long outer tentacles which are capable of catching insects approaching the size of a small housefly. Most form ground-hugging rosettes, but in a few a short stem is formed. In most species the centre of the rosette is protected from the dehydrating effect of strong sunlight by a silvery or whitish dome of bristle-like divisions of the stipules arising from the leaf bases. In winter, green to purple gemmae, or winter buds, are formed in the centre of the rosette instead of true leaves. Each gemma is seed-like, and when detached from its parent with a water-colour brush and placed on the surface of the compost, will soon produce leaves, root, and form a new plant.

The majority are easily grown in the coolhouse in a sunny position, using a compost of 1 part horticultural sand to 2 parts moss peat. The pot must be large enough to accommodate their hair-like, yet long, roots. For most species a 10cm (4in) pot will be large enough, and this will accommodate up to a dozen individuals, according to species. Keep the compost wet by using the tray system. Apply light shading to the glass in late spring.

Propagation is best by gemmae, placing each gemma just where you want the plant to mature. The best way of collecting gemmae from the parent plant is to hold the pot on its side and sweep them gently from the centre of the rosette with a sable brush, allowing them to fall safely on to a sheet of paper. They must be removed even if you do not wish to make use of them: if left they tend to 'suffocate' the centre of the rosette, often causing the death of the plant. Seed may also be used, but plants so raised take much longer to reach maturity.

A minority of species are more demanding, and as these include some particularly fine plants a little extra effort is justified. These often die back after flowering, especially if the weather is hot or if they are subjected to over-strong sunlight. This is a natural state of dormancy, but its disadvantage in cultivation is that it often leads to their death. Those most inclined to adopt this state are *DD. barbigera* (often called *D. drummondii*), *miniata*, *platystigma*, *pycnoblasta*, and the species 'Reagan's Ford' and 'Walyunga'.

These plants require firstly a very sandy compost – a little more than half of peat, the rest being of sand. A 12.5cm (5in) pot is suitable for most, but give *D. miniata* a 15cm (6in) pot.

AVOID DEHYDRATION

In summer, if they become dormant, the compost must be allowed to become dryish. The most obvious sign of impending dormancy is seen when the leaves have died halfway back. You must not allow the compost lower down in the pot to become too dry or you will lose your plants from dehydration. The secret is to maintain dampness in the lower part of the pot, while maintaining an apparently dry surface. Do this by standing the pot periodically in an inch of water for a few minutes. The frequency will depend entirely on the weather and climate. This can be done for three minutes during a very hot spell, but every

D adelae, red form, in flower and showing the characteristic curve of the flowering stalk

four days in cooler overcast weather.

For horticultural purposes, the pygmies can be divided into two groups: those which have minute foliage and proportionately small flowers, which I call true miniatures, and those which usually have larger or much larger foliage and with larger to proportionately very large flowers. Unless otherwise stated, the range of each species is limited to Western Australia.

Of the true miniatures perhaps, the tiniest is the Western Sundew *D. occidentalis*. Its flat, dark-red rosettes seldom exceed a diameter of 6mm (0.25in), about the length of a single tentacle on the Staghorn Sundew, and there is an attractive silvery white pyramid of stipules in the centre. The round blades scarcely ever exceed one millimetre in diameter, and the tentacles are so small that it is an excellent compliment to your eyesight if you can even see them, yet one glance through a x10 magnifying glass will confirm that this is an efficient insect catcher. The white flowers are singly borne and have rather narrow pointed petals.

The Pygmy Sundew *D. pygmaea* is eponymous to the group occurring in many parts of Australia, in Tasmania and New Zealand. It is larger, having rosettes 1cm (0.4in) across and roundish leaves. The whole plant is suffused with red, and soon forms rose-red colonies from seed and gemmae, providing brilliant backcloths to myriads of tiny four-petalled white flowers borne the summer long.

Still larger, forming rosettes to 14cm (5.5in) across, is the recently discovered *D.* sp. 'Beermullah' with dark reddish, but otherwise quite similar foliage, except for the conspicuous purple veins in each of its five white petals. *D.* sp. 'Lake Badgerup', is first-rate and should be in every collection. The rather larger rosettes are of a glowing coral pink. The leaves are upright when they are open, gradually becoming prostrate, giving the plant a globe-like form. Tight clumps form characteristic humps which become smothered with white starry flowers in high summer, making an attractive sight. In the typical form of the Shining Sundew *D. nitidula* the pinkish-green rosettes are up to 10mm (0.4in) across. It bears a cluster of several white flowers which are made more attractive by three large and club-like red stigmas. Several forms are in cultivation, including one which is larger in all its parts. Very similar is the Bright Sundew *D. omissa*, but in addition to botanical differences its foliage is bright golden green.

There is a wide range of colour amongst the larger pygmies. The Pretty Sundew *D. pulchella* in its typical form has rosettes to 15mm (0.6in) wide, the leaves being lettuce green with wide stalks and round blades, while the tentacles are red. Several flowers are borne per stalk, and these are pale pink, 8mm (0.3in) across. There is also an attractive giant form twice the size, with deep pink flowers, and a fine orange-flowered form. One of the finest introductions is undoubtedly *D.* sp. 'Bannister', found at the side of the Bannister road by Mr Philip Mann. The rosettes have narrower stalks but are otherwise very similar, but its chief glory is in its flowers. These are wide-petalled, of a delicious pearly pink, and up to as much as 15mm (0.6in) in diameter. They are produced through the greater part of the summer, and there are up to 30 to a scape. *D.* sp. 'Muchea Pink' has flowers of

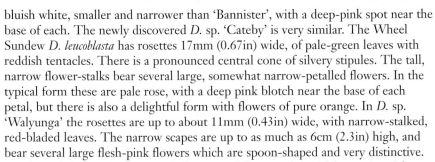

Left: The Notched Sundew *D. schizandra* is from the North Queensland rainforests

Above: The flowers of the Black-Eyed Sundew *D. platystigma* exceed the diameter of the entire plant

bluish white, smaller and narrower than 'Bannister', with a deep-pink spot near the base of each. The newly discovered *D.* sp. 'Cateby' is very similar. The Wheel Sundew *D. leucoblasta* has rosettes 17mm (0.67in) wide, of pale-green leaves with reddish tentacles. There is a pronounced central cone of silvery stipules. The tall, narrow flower-stalks bear several large, somewhat narrow-petalled flowers. In the typical form these are pale rose, with a deep pink blotch near the base of each petal, but there is also a delightful form with flowers of pure orange. In *D.* sp. 'Walyunga' the rosettes are up to about 11mm (0.43in) wide, with narrow-stalked, red-bladed leaves. The narrow scapes are up to as much as 6cm (2.3in) high, and bear several large flesh-pink flowers which are spoon-shaped and very distinctive.

The red-flowered species include some of the most beautiful pygmies. Of these, the Orange Sundew *D. miniata* is one of the finest, but is somewhat difficult to grow. Its short scape bears several flame-red, black-eyed flowers. A much easier plant to cultivate, with very similar flowers, is the *D.* sp. 'Brookton'. The petals are nearer to light vermilion-orange in colour, while the black area is less intense. The flowers of the Red Woolly Sundew *D. sewelliae* are flame red with black eyes, and the pin-headed stigmas are also black. The long red hairs on the flower buds no doubt account for its popular name. Drummond's Sundew *D. barbigera* (*D. drummondii*) is remarkable for the purity of its several bright orange-red flowers, which have black eyes. Unlike the previous reds, the leaf blades are not round but narrowly elliptical, and the plant gradually forms a very short stalk.

Amongst the white pygmies the Cone Sundew *D. androsacea* produces a rosette up to about 8mm (0.3in) across, with a ribbed silvery-white central cone, while the

Above: *Drosera sp.* 'Lake Badgerup' in its characteristically domed colony, next to a single plant

Centre: The flowers of the typical form of the Wheel Sundew *D. leucoblasta*, above the minute rosette

Above right: The Tall Sundew *D. auriculata* with its shield-shaped leaves and very long tentacles

large flowers have purplish veins. The Pearly Sundew *D. pycnoblasta* is so called because of the roundish mound of white stipules in the centre of the rosette of round-bladed, narrow-stalked leaves. The flowers are pure white. Some white-flowered species produce distinctive stalked rosettes while their petals are characteristically long and narrow. Of these, the Dwarf Sundew *D. paleacea* has rosettes to 12mm (0.47in). There are up to twelve flowers arranged on one side of the scape. Individually these seldom exceed 5.5mm (0.22in) in diameter. *D.* sp. 'Gingin Brook' has rather smaller flowers and rosettes, but the latter are borne on longer stems, while the flowering scapes are also taller, in *D.* sp. 'Armadale' the rosettes are about the same size as in *D. paleacea*, but up to eighteen flowers are borne on taller scapes and these are nearly three times as large, with a conspicuous greenish central vein down the middle of each petal.

The Shaggy Sundew *D. scorpioides* has rather larger rosettes of oar-shaped leaves, and up to thirty proportionately larger flowers. In the Rusty Sundew *D. dischrosepala* the stalked rosette is up to 2cm (0.8in) wide, and the creamy white flowers are arranged in a bouquet-like cluster at the top of the scape.

A newcomer, and up to twice the size, *D.* sp. 'Gidgegannup' has rather similar foliage arranged at somewhat eccentric angles with lovely apple-blossom pink flowers, several of which are borne on one side of a hairy scape. There is also a white form.

Of other colours, the Black-Eyed Sundew *D. platystigma* is a beauty, with short scapes of up to seven large black-eyed flowers in a delicious shade of pure soft orange. The rosettes of round-bladed leaves are up to 11mm (0.43in) across. *D.* sp. 'Reagan's Ford' is possibly unique among pygmies in its large canary-yellow flowers. The base of the petals is white. This is a lovely species which has been confused with the white-flowered *D. pycnoblasta*.

The Scarlet Sundew *D. glanduligera* should rightly be included here, although it is an annual. The rosettes are of a yellowish green and there are up to twenty flowers to the scape. The flowers are rather small and bright red. It comes easily from seed, but can fail to grow to maturity.

THE TUBEROUS SUNDEWS

Quite different from all the other species are those which form tubers. All are natives to Australasia and most come from Western Australia. The tubers allow the plants to survive arid conditions. Growth usually starts in autumn when the ground may still be bone-dry, but nourishment necessary for growth is supplied by the tuber from which the new season's shoot grows. By the time this penetrates the surface the winter rains may have already begun. It is during this period that growth is most active, and in the dual requirements of extreme wetness and infertile soil these species do not differ much from others. The plant continues to draw upon the food reserves in the old tuber, but at the same time is building up a new one. The plants usually flower when the rains have ceased and the ground gradually dries out. As it does so, seed is formed and the plant itself starts to die back to its newly formed tuber. It remains dormant during the summer, shooting into growth in autumn to repeat the process. The tuberous species can be divided into three groups of differing appearances, the Rainbow, the Rosetted Tuberous and the Fan Sundews.

THE RAINBOW SUNDEWS

These form tough wire-like stems which can be upright and erect, branching and shrub-like, arching or climbing, according to species. The leaves are small and dainty, seldom exceeding 3mm (0.12in) across. Some are round and semicircular, others are shield-shaped, and these often have lynx-ear-like lobes from each corner, which are crowned with extra-long tentacles. The flowers are several to many on terminal stalks, are white, pink or occasionally yellow, and can be very showy. Some require a high degree of understanding and skill in their cultivation, others are easy to grow, and these include some of the best. Grow them in a compost of one-third horticultural sand to two-thirds moss peat, in a sunny position in the coolhouse. Plant the tubers three times deeper than their own thickness. Keep the compost just moist during dormancy, but water on the tray system from the emergence of growth until the plant shows clear signs of dying back. All are Western Australian unless otherwise stated. One of the easiest to grow is the Pale Sundew *D. peltata*, found across Southern China, India, Japan, South-East Asia and the east of Australia. It is erect, single-stemmed or occasionally branching to 25cm (10in), with shield-shaped green or reddish leaves, and a cluster of medium sized white to pink flowers. It is an attractive plant and is raised from seed. Use a 10cm (4in) pot or 12.5cm (5in) dwarf pot. The Tall Sundew *D. auriculata* may also be found from Brisbane to South Australia and in Tasmania and New Zealand. It is very similar to *D. peltata*, and identical treatment suits it. There is both a white and a pink form.

The tree-like Giant Sundew *D. gigantea* coming into flower. Almost every leaf has caught a victim

The Giant Sundew *D. gigantean* may exceed 1m (40in) in the wild, and is as attractive as it is impressive. Larger plants are much branched, and give the impression of miniature trees. The leaves are small and shield-shaped, and the plant is at its best when seen scattered, with its white flowers. Easy from seed, but seedlings may take years to reach a large size. Tubers 1cm (0.4in) or larger should be planted in 20cm (8in) pots. The Pink Sundew *D. menziesii* has several large flowers to 3cm (1.2in) across, in shades from a beautiful apricot through rose to deep reddish-pink. It can be scrambling or erect, the leaves bronzy to reddish, and the height 10–36cm (4–14in) according to the form. At the onset of dormancy give this species six weeks without water, afterwards keeping the compost damp and treating as for the previous species. The pot size will, of course, depend on the size of the form you grow, but if in doubt give it a 12.5cm (5in) pot. A break in colour from other species is provided by the Sulphur Flowered Sundew *D. sulphurea*, with erect zig-zagging stems to 35.5cm (14in), lobed leaves and several brilliant-yellow flowers as much as 25mm (1in) in diameter.

Other Rainbow species are not for the beginner. The vital factor is that they should be dried out soon after the first signs of oncoming dormancy are evident, and the pots must remain dry until growth re-emerges. Treat exactly as recommended for the rosetted species below, except that they must be planted at least three times deeper than their tuber size. The Bridal Sundew *D. macrantha* climbs to to 91cm (36in), with large white scented flowers; the Sunny Rainbow *D. subhirtella*, grows to 50cm (20in), another climber with red-tinted leaves and large yellow flowers; the Erect Sundew *D. stricticaulis* to 30cm (12in), with golden leaves and large rosy flowers; the Jewel Rainbow *D. neesii*, like a taller version of the last but with lobed leaves; the Swamp Rainbow *D. heterophylla* to 30cm (12in), with lovely many-petalled flowers and kidney-shaped leaves; the Fringed Sundew *D. thysanosepala*, semi-climbing to 38cm (15in) with semicircular reddish leaves and rose-pink flowers; the Modest Rainbow *D. modesta*, a climber to 92cm (36in) with yellowish-green lobed leaves and very large white flowers; and the Purple Sundew *D. microphylla* to 33cm (13in), unusual in that its purplish-pink petals are held within a 'cup' of extra-large green sepals.

THE ROSETTED SUNDEWS

These form flat rosettes which differ from those of other rosette-forming species in two respects. Firstly the number of leaves produced for one growing season is limited, so that no small immature foliage is later seen in the centre of the rosette, and secondly, after the flowering period the existing foliage suddenly undergoes a second spate of growth and greatly increases in size. The magnificent rosettes form their main attraction, but all have showy flowers. These were once considered to be difficult plants, and although they are not easy, the main key to success is to dry out the pots at exactly the right time.

The compost dries out most rapidly in smaller pots. In all cases a 10cm (4in) size is ideal. Use 2 parts silver sand to 1 part moss pear. Never attempt to dig up a plant unless it is dormant. Newly acquired or dug-up tubers should be kept in small clip-tight closed polythene bags to prevent dehydration, and must not be replanted until a small shoot is seen forming at the top of the tuber. It is then ready for potting. The tuber should be firmly potted and positioned so that its crown is about 15mm (0.6in) below the surface of the compost, but you should at this stage keep the crown temporarily exposed by means of an excavation. Then place the pot in about 2.5cm (1in) of water until the surface of the compost is visibly moist, when it must be removed. Now run a little silver sand over the exposed crown of the tuber, sufficient to cover all but the growing-point of the shoot. Place the pot in a sunny place in the coolhouse, and keep the compost just moist. As the shoot grows, scatter on more sand, always leaving the growing-point exposed, and repeat this either until the excavation is filled, or until the leaf rosette starts to expand at the end of the shoot. When the leaf rosette starts to expand the careful system of watering is no longer necessary, and the pot can be placed in the water tray in a sunny position. Leave until the onset of dormancy is indicated by the yellowing or browning of the foliage. Immediately remove the pot from the water tray and allow it to dry out. It can be placed under the staging once the leaves have completely died away, but do not remove it from the greenhouse, as it is important that the air is still reasonably humid to prevent too much loss of water by the tuber during dormancy, even though the compost must be dry.

When at last new growth is seen emerging from the compost, place the pot immediately in the water tray, for now that it is established in its pot there is no need to repeat the settling-in process. In several years' time the tubers may reach the bottom of the pot, as they tend to reform at a lower level annually. They are likely to die due to excessive wet at the level of the water tray, and to avoid this happening it is advisable to repot every three years. These are the only sundews which I feel benefit from artificial fertilizer, though this must always be applied as a light spray and never directly to the soil. Use the same fertilizer and dilution as for *Nepenthes* (see page 125).

D. erythrorhiza and no doubt other species can be propagated by seed, though this may take up to three years to germinate. It should be sown in late summer or early autumn, remembering that these are winter growers. Thin or transplant to about 2.5cm (1in) apart when large enough to handle. When transplanting make quite sure that the entire root system is intact. Treat the dormant seed and seedlings just as you would the adult plants (the pots of seed which has not yet germinated should be dried off at exactly the time you would in the case of adult plants, beginning watering again at the same time also). Adventitious tubers are formed underground in established plants; these ultimately form clumps which can be divided during dormancy when repotting, which is probably the best means of propagation for the amateur.

With one exception all rosetted sundews are natives to Western Australia. Of these, the Red Ink Sundew *D. erythrorhiza* is available in a variety of distinct

The Scented Sundew *D. whittakeri* is probably the easiest rosetted sundew to cultivate

forms. In some forms the rosettes of roundish leaves may reach a diameter of up to 15cm (6in) after flowering. In one, the leaves are attractively variegated in bands of red and green. All bear heads of many medium-sized white flowers on single stems. The Snowy Sundew *D. macrophylla* has rosettes of up to eight obovate leaves. Several to many flowering stalks each bear up to three large white flowers. The Red-Leaved Sundew *D. bulbosa* seems self-descriptive from its popular name, but there are also green-leaved forms. It has large rosettes of roundish leaves and usually several flowering scapes, each bearing one large white flower. A particularly shy flowerer is the Painted Sundew *D. zonaria*, but its chief charm is in its kidney-shaped leaves, which are emerald green beautifully fringed with a red band. In nature it seems only to produce its white flowers after a bush fire.

Two of the plants discovered by Allan Lowrie appear to be distinct species: *D.* sp. 'Purnta' with its spoon-shaped leaves in red and green in three sizes, gives the intriguing effect of three distinct rosettes arranged one within the other. *D.* sp. 'Mogumber' has unusually shaped leaves. The blade is orb-shaped and is held on a long stalk. Both have white flowers.

The Scented Sundew *D. whittakeri* is the easiest of all rosetted species to grow. It somewhat resembles *D. erythrorhiza*, but is smaller. It differs from other species in being native only to Victoria and South Australia. It can be grown in a good light in a frost-proof greenhouse (coolhouse), with up to seven tubers in a 12.5cm (5in) pot. Use 1 part moss spear to 2 parts silver sand and water by the tray system, keeping the compost moist even during dormancy. Its tolerance, or even requirement, of moisture at this time is clearly due to the very different climates that it experiences in nature; if you try keeping the Western Australian rosetted species permanently wet you will certainly lose them. Propagate from seed.

Drosera binata var. *multifida*

THE FAN SUNDEWS

These sundews have thick, leafy, usually branching stems. The sturdy fan-shaped leaf blades have wide stalks which clasp the stem. Cultivate them as you would the rosetted sundews. The Leafy Sundew *D. stolonifera* is perhaps the most attractive. It occurs in several forms, all of which are worth growing. The leaves are arranged up the stems in whorls of three or four. 'Branching Form' has branching stems to about 15cm (6in), giving a miniature shrub-like effect. Its leaves are green with red glands, and the large white flowers are slender-petalled. In 'Upright Form' there is a single erect stem, reddish foliage and white flowers. The variety *D. stolonifera humilis* is dwarf. 'Alpine Form', the dwarf discovered by Allan Lowrie, differs from all these in having pink flowers set upon reddish leaves and foliage. *D. ramellosa* is few-stemmed and sprawling to semi-upright, with stems up to 10cm (4in) long, with golden-green leaves and white flowers. *D. platypoda* has single stems up to 25cm (10in), which may branch towards the top, and is reputed to produce its white flowers only after a bush fire the previous year.

The Trumpet Pitchers: Sarracenia

The Yellow Trumpet *S. flava* typifies the upright-pitchered *Sarracenia* species. This is a veined form

Shaped like single horns or trumpets, the pitchers are surmounted at the back by lid-like 'hoods'. The large nodding flowers appear on long straight stems in spring, and somewhat resemble peonies. They consist of five petal-like sepals and five petals which overhang a curious object like an upside-down umbrella. This is part of the pistil where pollen collects, which has been released from the stamens above, and in nature this is unwittingly transferred from one flower to another on the bodies of visiting bumble bees.

Cultivation All the species covered in this book, their subspecies and hybrids will grow well in the coolhouse, with one exception. This is *S. purpurea* ssp. *purpurea*, which prefers cooler temperatures. They may also be grown satisfactorily outside in warm temperate to sub-tropical climates, providing the tray system of watering is used, or if they are planted in a bog garden (see page 20).

The hardier species, *SS. purpurea* ssp. *purpurea*, *flava*, *rubra* ssp. *jonesii*, *oreophila*, and the hybrids between these species will put up with some degree of frost, so can be grown in unheated greenhouses in many cool temperate areas, providing winter ventilation is adequate. This means leaving greenhouse doors and ventilators open during the average day, only closing them during freezing periods and at night. Again, the hardier species will be found hardy in the artificial bog outdoors in many temperate areas, but though the hardiness of *S. purpurea* ssp. *purpurea* is certain, others mentioned still need to be tested in colder districts. Some make good subjects for sunny window-sills (see page 46).

Start your collection with well-grown, mature plants rather than with young plants or seed. Not only may it take years for a young plant to reach maturity (five to seven years from seed is normal), but a mature plant is much less likely to be lost in the hands of the beginner. A 12.5cm (5in) pot will be large enough for most mature species and hybrids, except for very large growers such as *S. flava* 'Maxima' and *S. moorei* 'Marston Clone'. For 'Marston Clone' use a 15cm (6in) pot.

In the case of *S. psittacina* use a 12.5cm (5in) dwarf pot which is easier to submerge in water in winter. Do not to use either pure peat or a compost based on sphagnum moss, for both cause microconditions which encourage attack from common Grey Mould (*Botrytis cinerea*). A good combination is 4 parts moss peat, 2 parts seed grade Perlite, and 1 part horticultural sand. Mix the sand well with the peat before mixing with the Perlite. The result is an open mixture which will not sour, and can be used for all species and hybrids except *S. psittacina*, which requires a mix of 3 parts moss peat to 1 part horticultural sand, as Perlite will float during the submerged period.

Potting should be done in spring, just as the young pitchers are shooting from the rhizome, for it is mainly then that the new roots are formed. Never do this in late summer, autumn or winter, for the plants cannot then easily re-establish themselves and are quite likely to die. Crocks should not be used. Planting should be firm. Spread out the roots and ensure that the top half only of the rhizome is above soil level. The crown should be at or just above surface level. Planting the plant deeper will often cause winter rot. An exception is *S. minor*, where the rhizome should always be just below surface level. After planting, lightly sprinkle the growing point with water to wash away any loose compost.

The Yellow Trumpet *S. flava* produces magnificent flowers in spring or early summer

Yellow Trumpet forms. Shown in the picture from left to right are 'Heavily Veined', 'Copper Lid' and 'Red' forms. The seed head is characteristically raised after petal fall

The plants should be watered on the tray system, with the partial exception of *S. psittacina* which prefers the tray system in summer, but in autumn, place it in a deep container of soft water so that the pitchers are just submerged. This not only to some degree reproduces the flooding to which it is often subjected in nature, but protects it from the attack of grey mould to which the species is peculiarly prone during winter.

Place the plants in a sunny position, and apply light shading to the glass in late spring, removing this in autumn. Do not let the hoods of the pitchers get too near the glass of the roof, as this can often cause their edges to wither and die ('pitcher-burn'). The same may happen if you do not water by the tray system and allow the compost to become a little too dry.

The pitchers always catch sufficient insects for the nourishment of the plant, even if they are grown in apparently 'fly-free' houses. In the cases of the two *S. purpurea* subspecies alone, a little water should be maintained in each pitcher during the summer only, as a substitute for the rain they would normally collect which is essential for overcoming their prey. Never use any type of fertilizer, which will cause root decay and will almost certainly kill your plant.

Regularly remove dead growth as it can lead to disease. As the pitchers or phyllodes (flattened leaf-like structures which develop at the end of summer in some species) die back, simply cut the dead parts off with scissors, leaving the live part intact, for this is still valuable to the plant. When a leaf has entirely died back, see that every bit of it is removed with scissors. Occasionally, in summer, a part of the pitcher tube may die as a result of 'indigestion', because more insects than the plant's digestive juices could cope with were caught at one time. In this case it is unnecessary to cut back the pitcher at all unless the entire pitcher above this zone dies. This phenomenon often occurs in nature in upright-pitchered species, and does not normally harm the plant. Apart from this, the plants will need remarkably little attention other than the topping-up of the water tray.

Propagation Sarracenias can be increased by division, rhizome cuttings and seed. Division is the simplest method, and must be done in spring, just as the young pitchers are coming into growth. You should not attempt to divide your plant until it has formed a large lump of four or more individual rhizome branches, two to four years after potting because the younger, less-well-developed crowns will have few if any roots at that stage, so will either take a long time to establish themselves or be unsuitable for use. The longer you keep your plant the faster it will tend to produce suitable growth for division.

To divide, first gently knock the plant out of the pot and remove the compost which falls away without damaging the roots. Remove the rest by rinsing the plant in a bucket of water, so the roots are not damaged and the rhizomes are exposed. You will now be able to see clearly which of the rhizome branches have developed roots and are therefore suitable division material. Often these will break off from the parent rhizome easily and without damage, but otherwise cut cleanly with a sharp knife. Plant in the same sized pot as the parent plant grows in.

Rhizome cuttings Again, this method should be used only in the spring, when you are repotting or dividing the parent plant. You will often find unnecessarily long rhizomes which have no live roots – those attached are from previous years and are mere anchors; they are of no use to the plant other than as survival mechanisms after fires in the wild. Providing your plant is left with 2.5cm (1in) or so of rhizome you can remove the remainder with a clean cut. The far end of this will be old and possibly dead.

Remove all this old dead area, carefully cutting off section after thin section until you see no more brown dead growth and the interior is seen to be all creamy white and live. If the remaining rhizome is long enough it can be cut into two or more cuttings, each being about 2.5cm (1in) long. Pot the cuttings in standard *Sarracenia* compost. A 15cm (6in) dwarf pot will accommodate up to seven without overcrowding. Bury these horizontally to half their depth in the compost, but first ensure that each is the right way up, which is usually self-evident from the position of the old root. Plant firmly, and afterwards mound a little compost against both ends of each cutting so that the cut is not exposed. Place out of direct sunlight but in a good light, and water on the tray system. Note that a dryish compost, a low humidity, strong sunlight and a high temperature can all singly or in combination be the causes of the collapse of these cuttings. Growing buds take anything from weeks to months to appear, but the 'take' is often high, and some cuttings can develop several crowns. Some cuttings may produce mature plants within little more than a year's time.

Rhizome notching is a variation on rhizome cuttings. Its advantage is that dormant buds are forced into growth on old rhizomes without the need to disturb the parent plant in any way. Moreover, the growth is usually faster and the success rate often higher. It can only be done where the rhizome is of an accessible kind, an excellent method in the cases of *S. leucophylla* and *S. oreophila*, in which the rhizomes are usually exposed on the surface.

Cut a notch out of the top of the rhizome with a sharp knife. This should be at least 2.5 cm (1in) behind the growing point of the rhizome, and no more than half the depth of the rhizome. Before you do this it may be necessary to remove a little compost from either side of the rhizome to prevent this from polluting the notch. Do not substitute a single cut for a notch, as this can often lead to infection, and do not completely sever the rhizome as this reduces the success rate. Notching usually results in a clump of new growth occurring on the old rhizome, and ultimately each new crown will produce roots, at which stage they should be detached and potted.

Seed is mature only when the seed capsule has become dead and brown in autumn. It provides the best method of obtaining large supplies of a species, but be warned that the seedlings will take from five to seven years to reach maturity. Hybrids will not reproduce true from seed; nor will individual selected cultivars, be they of hybrids or of species. It is incorrect for anyone to supply seed claiming to be, say, *S. x* 'Evendine', or *S. flava* 'Maxima'. Distributing seed gathered from a

The White Trumpet *S. leucophylla*

named clone even if the clonal name is not used, may result in some seedlings which could be mistaken for the cultivar and thus lead to confusion with, and the eventual loss of, the true clone.

The seed should be less than a year old, and is best sown in late winter or early spring. After a year its ability to germinate (its viability) rapidly deteriorates, and it should then be dampened and placed into the main compartment of the fridge for a fortnight before sowing. Do this in any case to all seed from commercial sources or other seed that cannot be checked for freshness, as this seems to nudge a much higher proportion of stale seeds into germination. Do not freeze!

Sow for preference in coolhouse, or otherwise similar conditions, on the surface of a standard *Sarracenia* compost in plastic seed boxes or dwarf pots. Spray with Benomyl or Captan against fungal attack. Now dry some moss peat thoroughly on a warm surface and shake some through a fine kitchen sieve onto the seeds until they disappear from view (i.e. are hardly covered at all). This microscopically thin layer will act as a further shield to fungal spores, and as an additional precaution, spray this layer itself with the fungicide. Place in the water tray in shallow soft water. You should see signs of germination in around six weeks' time. Leave the seedlings in the box until they have produced about three pitchers each, and then prick them out. Never do this in autumn or winter, as this will result in losses. Use a deeper container at this stage, plastic cat-litter trays with several drainage holes bored in the bottom are excellent. Use standard *Sarracenia* compost except for *S. psittacina*. The latter should be pricked out into the same peat and sand mixture recommended for the mature plant, and similarly the seedling plants should be submerged each winter.

When digging up the seedlings be careful to dig deeply enough to ensure that the root systems are undamaged, and in pricking out make a hole with a mini-dibber deep enough to ensure that they go directly downwards and are not doubled back or cramped. Gently firm, and space at least 2.5cm (1in) apart. They can remain in situ until they approach maturity and show signs of becoming overcrowded, in two to three years' time, when they should be potted as recommended for the mature plants.

Pests In nature several interesting pests occur which are peculiar to these plants, but you are unlikely to encounter these if you buy well-grown nursery-grown material, where pests are relatively few in number and easily controlled. Greenfly (*Aphis*) often attack young growth, resulting in often seriously distorted pitchers. They are easily controlled with any greenhouse or houseplant aphicide. Scale insects can also prove a nuisance, and will cause unsightly Sooty Mould to grow on the honeydew that they secrete. If they are few in number they may be removed with a cloth dipped in warm water with a little detergent added. Spray the plant afterwards with a suitable systematic insecticide, such as Dimethoate. On a larger scale several sprays at weekly intervals may be necessary. Woodlice, which can do much damage to the rhizomes and roots, will often kill them by causing the wounds in which grey mould can get a foothold. They come out at night, when it is a good plan to spray not only the pots but the entire greenhouse with liquid Pyrethrum insecticide, two or three applications at fortnightly intervals being usually necessary. Alternatively, they may be gathered by laying traps of scooped-out potato halves placed upside-down on the compost surface. Millipedes also attack rhizomes, though more occasionally. These are too often confused with the beneficial centipedes: centipedes have flat bodies, one pair of legs per segment, and run away when disturbed. The dangerous millipede has a long, rounded, usually darkish body, two pairs of legs per segment, and curls up when disturbed. They are easily got rid of with any good soil pesticide. Leatherjackets, the larvae of the cranefly or daddy-long-legs (*Tipula* spp.) can cripple plants grown out of doors, and occasionally those grown in the greenhouse, by eating the roots. Again, a soil pesticide will usually eliminate them. They are rarely found in greenhouses in which large clumps of Fork-Leaved Sundews are grown, as these catch the adult flies with remarkable efficiency.

Diseases The only serious one likely to affect any of your plants is the common Grey Mould (*Botrytis cinerea*), easily recognizable for it is very similar to the mould that occurs on old damp bread. It is usually found on the rhizome of the plant, around the base of the leaves, or in the growing point. In summer it occasionally remains localized on the rhizome, and can even die out, but more often it advances, ultimately killing the plant and this is almost invariably so in winter attacks. Prevention is better than cure, and this is a disease which seldom causes trouble once you have learned the precautions to take against its occurrence. As mentioned earlier, sphagnum-moss-based composts encourage it. This is because they tend to set up microclimates around the dead leaf bases which encourage the germination of the mould spores and nurture the young mycelia. Soggy peat, which has not been mixed with materials to make it open (see page 8), has a similar effect. The mould almost invariably establishes itself on dead tissues before invading live tissue, so be particularly careful to remove as much dead growth from the plant as you can. Also ensure strict hygiene in the house by removing all dead material from it which is likely to be a source of infection.

Always avoid wetting the crown and exposed parts of the rhizome in autumn, winter and early spring, as this may cause germination of any spores that lodge there. Ensure that all shading wash or material is removed from the glass during the same period, as the fungus thrives in a low light. Even when you have taken these precautions you may still have trouble with plants which have formed thick clumps of growth, especially in the case of large plants of the typical form of *S. rubra*. This is because the conditions within the clump consist of shade, little air movement and high humidity, a combination which especially favours the fungus. It is therefore wise to divide in spring any clumps that are likely otherwise to become over-large by autumn.

In addition to the above precautions a good preventative measure is to spray at monthly intervals during autumn and winter with a good systematic fungicide such as Benomyl. If you have a plant that has been attacked, the infected area must be

Yellow Trumpet 'Burgundy' form

removed. If this is near the base of a leaf it may be possible to cut this off low before it reaches the rhizome. However, if it is already in the rhizome more drastic surgery will be necessary. Use a sharp knife and attempt to cut the affected area out. If you can see a brown area within the flesh of the rhizome, here you may assume that this, too, is affected. This should be cut away by cutting straight through the rhizome and removing one or more cross-sections until there is no sign at all of dead growth, taking an extra section as a precaution.

It may be that you are left with a short length of older rhizome and a separate length of new rhizome with a growing point, with only one or the other, or at worst nothing at all. If left with some old rhizome it can be expected to shoot in weeks or months as if it were a rhizome cutting.

Sooty Mould *Fumago* spp. can hardly be called a disease of the plant, since it does not live in its tissues but on it. It is harmless but very unsightly, causing a black soot-like deposit over the foliage. You will often find it at its worst during an infection of scale insects or aphids, when it lives on the honeydew secreted by them. In such cases the logical control is first to destroy the pests, and then remove the mould. This can be done with a cloth and warm water with a little detergent added. Moisten the pitcher first, and after a couple of minutes the mould can be gently wiped away. It also sometimes grows on the nectar secreted by the pitcher, when it spoils the appearance. It thrives when the plants are exposed to bright sunlight under glass. It is not usually troublesome if shading is applied to the glass in late spring.

THE SPECIES
The upright-pitchered kinds contain some of the most elegant plants. The forwardly inclined hood helps to exclude rain and acts as a tempting yet highly dangerous feeding ground for its insect visitors. The Yellow Trumpet *S. flava* is one of the most beautiful and occurs in wet savannahs the south-east US. It bears in spring large and lovely brimstone flowers up to 10cm (4in) wide, which possess a bitter-sweet fragrance, and these are followed by slender pitchers from 46cm (18in) to over 76cm (30in), according to form.

In this, as in other species, long-imbibing insects seem to show increasing signs of intoxication as they feed, becoming increasingly less shy and more and more unsteady on their legs. That many lose their footing to the advantage of the plant as a result of their incapacity is obvious. Interestingly enough, a drug, coniine, has been separated from this species. Administered in tiny quantities to fire ants, its effect was first to narcotise and ultimately to kill each ant.

In late summer the plant produces flat non-carnivorous leaves called phyllodes. These are its winter leaves which persist after the pitchers have died down in autumn. It makes a fine plant for the sunny window-sill, adapting well to these conditions. A useful one, too, for it will effectively control houseflies, bluebottles, and even the occasional wasp, which may save you the use of expensive and possibly toxic sprays and the like. Dr Donald Schnell has identified the following

five distinct variants in the wild, which are all now in cultivation. Both in nature and in horticulture you will find an endless range of hybrids of differing complexity between these.

In the 'Typical Form' there is a yellow to yellow-green background colour to the upper pitcher and hood, with a large splotch of deep maroon within the centre of the column of the hood from which a few faint to moderate red veins radiate. It is perhaps seen at its best in the typical Gulf Coast form, often referred to as *S. flava* var. *rugelii*, in which the golden-green pitchers are very large and the

The Yellow Trumpet *S. flava* 'Heavily Veined' form

Yellow Trumpets *S. flava* in the Florida
Panhandle

splotch has few noticeable radiating red veins. The 'Heavily-Veined' form has a
yellow to golden-green background colour and almost all the pitcher is heavily
veined in dark red. The hood is rather broad and undulates irregularly. In the
'Copper Lid' form the outer surface of the hood, column, and sometimes the
upper quarter of the pitcher too are distinctively tinted with copper-red, and the
upper pitcher is moderately veined in dark red. In the 'Red' forms almost the
entire outside of the pitcher is coloured red to maroon, while the inner surface
and nectar roll is yellowish-green to yellow. In shade the red becomes paler, and

strong red veins are then evident. Two good forms which have found their way
into cultivation are 'Burgundy', a great beauty, in which the outer pitcher tube is
plum red, the nectar roll soft yellow, while the hood is yellow-green, strongly
veined in red; and 'Claret', which is also attractive, with long slender pitchers
tinted maroon and strongly veined in darker colour, giving way to the yellowish-
green background colour towards the mouth and in the hood. I was shown a pure
stand of this form extending to many acres in the Florida Panhandle. This was
scheduled for drainage and afforestation, and I believe the solitary seedling which I
rescued at the timed has been the source of all the European stock.

Most of the *S. flava* at present cultivated in Europe is of hybrid stock, and is to
some degree veined in red. The vigorous selected clone *S. flava* var. 'Maxima' is
such a one. In it the pitchers are well formed and large, usually about 75cm (30in)
tall or more. The upper part of the pitcher and the lid are golden-green, the latter
being semicircular with, generally, hardly any spur, and lightly veined and
splotched with maroon within, while the lower part of the pitcher and the
phyllodes have a characteristic blue-grey tint. There is a mistaken belief that
large-growing plants in the wild – they can reach 120cm (4ft) – can be called by
this name. This is not so, nor can seedlings of the variety itself, but only
vegetatively propagated material, a point which holds true with all clonal varieties
in plants. The variety 'Marston Dwarf' is of my own selection and has heavily
veined pitchers seldom exceeding 31cm (12in) in height. It soon forms clumps,
and is a useful and attractive plant for small sunny windows.

NEAR EXTINCTION
The Green Pitcher Plant *S. oreophila* could easily be mistaken for a smaller edition
of Yellow Trumpet with green pitchers. However, distinct differences are to be
found in the mouth, which tends to be rounder, the lip tends to be on one level
and lacks the frontal 'spout' of the *S. flava*. *In addition*, the hood which tends to be
more erect with an almost vertical column. But the flat winter leaves provide the
most obvious difference when not in flower. These are much shorter, and instead
of being more or less straight and upright, are inclined sideways, the upper part
being bent downwards and round into a pronounced sickle shape. The flowers
resemble *S. flava* in form, but are yellowish-green and have a sweet fragrance.
The plant is regrettably nearing extinction in its limited range in the southern
Appalachian Mountains, due to agricultural activities and unscrupulous collectors.
While I do not rate this as one of the more beautiful species it has an
extraordinary property when used as a parent in the raising of hybrids. Though
relatively small-growing itself, its hybrid offspring often possess remarkable
vigour, are often larger than either parent, and can become relative giants.

The slender pitchers of the White Trumpet *S. leucophylla* usually reach 76cm
(30in), but can exceed 92cm (36in) in height. The upper pitcher and lid are white
with a netting of veins in green, maroon or red. The netting may be extremely
finely pencilled or it may be broad, and in no two seedlings will you find the pattern

A colony of Yellow Trumpets in the
Florida Panhandle

The Pale Trumpet *S. alata*. The flowers vary from creamy yellow to pure white

of coloration exactly similar. In addition to an early summer crop of pitchers, another is formed in early autumn, while in late summer a limited number of winter leaves are often, but not always, produced. Beautiful as the pitchers are, the flowers held on tall slender stems are of an intense shade of ruby red with a slight scent of violets. A southerner, from Georgia, North Florida and the Gulf Coast.

In the Pale Trumpet *S. alata* the flowers are distinct from all others in being the softest creamy yellow to pure white. They make a lovely contrast when grouped with other species. Again, the pitchers are sometimes confused with those of the Yellow Trumpet. However, they are narrower, the mouth slopes markedly to the front, and the hood is narrower and overlaps at a much lower angle. Pale green while young the pitcher usually becomes a yellowish-green, sometimes reddening with age. The outside of the tube is strongly marked with dark red, longitudinal veins. These become finely netted in the upper part, which is continued into the hood. There are no winter leaves. In some desirable forms part or all of the inner sides of the column and hood are deep red. This species extends westwards in a broken range along the Gulf Coast from Alabama, and is the only species which crosses the Texan border.

In some varieties of the Sweet Trumpet *S. rubra* the pitchers bear a passing resemblance to those of the Pale Trumpet, but they can easily be distinguished by the colour of their sweetly scented flowers. Soft Indian red to maroon, they vary much in size amongst the subspecies.

The narrow pitchers tend to be floppy when first produced in spring, but those produced in summer are upright. *S. rubra* ssp. *rubra* is the typical form, and occurs in the Carolinas and northern Georgia. The pitchers are up to 45cm (18in) in their largest forms, but usually smaller. They are narrow with a wide wing. The rim of the mouth curves strongly upwards until it meets the short column of the hood, which is elliptical, pointed, and curves forwards over the mouth. They are at first green, the upper part and lid soon becoming bronzy to coppery in hue with finely pencilled, maroon longitudinal veins. The flowers are up to 4.5cm (1.77in) across, and are the smallest in the genus, those of the other *S. rubra* subspecies also being larger.

The Mountain Pitcher Plant *S. rubra* ssp. *jonesii* occurs rarely in the mountains in the west of North and South Carolina. The pitchers are much taller and more robust, to about 60cm (24in). The mouth is expanded, while the hood has a more pronounced column and is wider. The veins are often distinctly purple. *S. rubra* ssp. *gulfensis* occurs only in one area of the Florida Panhandle. The pitchers are usually about the same length and as robust as ssp. *jonesii*, but otherwise resemble more a larger edition of ssp. *rubra*.

The Alabama Canebrake Pitcher *S. rubra* ssp. *alabamensis* is restricted in range to central Alabama. The pitcher is up to 49cm (19in), and is distinguishable from other subspecies in being much paler, the copper tinting and maroon coloration of veins often being nearly or completely absent. The mouth is wider than in others too, the hood is altogether larger with a distinctly wavy margin, and the pitcher is

S. rubra ssp. *jonesii* is a mountain dwelling subspecies of the Sweet Trumpet

far more reminiscent of a young Yellow Trumpet than of the typical *S. rubra*. Also from a restricted range in Alabama, *S. rubra* ssp. *wherryi* somewhat resembles the last in form alone, but the pitchers that grow to about 43cm (17in) are rather shorter and narrower in tube and hood, while in coloration and in its conspicuously pencilled maroon veins it closely resembles the typical *S. rubra*.

In the Hooded Pitcher Plant *S. minor* we see a departure from all other upright-pitchered species, for in this the domed hood forms a perfect canopy over the mouth, while the back part of this dome and of the upper pitcher is thickly

S. X 'DANIEL RUDD'

The earlier artificially produced *Sarracenia* hybrids were mainly a result of hybridisation for its own sake; if two species or hybrids were in flower at one time the temptation was to cross them, then efforts were first made to breed plants of outstanding quality and beauty.

The very best of the seedlings of such carefully conceived crosses – say, one in 3,000 – should be selected and named, since this is the only way it is likely to be preserved. *S. x 'Daniel Rudd'* is a vigorous *S. x catesbaei*, in which a parent *S. flava* 'Maxima' was crossed with *S. leucophylla*. Most of the resulting seedlings were attractive, but one was vastly superior to all others and seemed to possess every good quality, and it appears to have an excellent constitution.

The upper pitcher and hood are at first pleasantly marbled in light green, later becoming tinged with coppery chestnut and darker veins, and they have the advantage over most upright-pitchered kinds in that they often open when the plant is still in flower. The deep-red flowers appear on long straight stems, and may remain in petal for as long as twenty-one days.

scattered with oval translucent 'windows'. These serve an excellent purpose, for they are mistaken for exits by insect visitors, which having made this error are almost certain to fall for ever into the abyss below. In the typical form the pitchers may be as short as 23cm (9in) in some plants, reaching to 46cm (18in) in others. It occurs from South Carolina to mid-Florida, further south than any other *Sarracenia*. In the Okefenokee Swamp around the Georgia-Florida border there is a unique giant form which, unlike the typical form which grows in the drier parts of bogs, usually occurs in up to 60cm (2ft) of water. Here, I saw myself, the length of the pitcher above water-level is up to 91cm (3ft), and must be much longer if the portion beneath is added. The rather small flowers are of clear cadmium yellow. The remaining two species differ considerably from the other six in habit. In the Huntsman's Cup *S. purpurea* the drinking-horn-shaped pitchers rest in rosettes upon the ground, thence curving upwards to the wide horizontal mouth. The lid is unique amongst the trumpets in being vertical, so that rather than excluding rain it allows its entry. It makes use of the accumulated water both in overcoming its prey and in its digestion, for within this medium bacteria multiply and assist the plant's digestive juices in breaking down the bodies of its victims.

SUBSPECIES

The Northern Pitcher Plant *S. purpurea* ssp. *purpurea* has a huge range from New Jersey northwards and north-westerly over the Canadian border into arctic regions. As one would expect, it is extremely hardy. It has been naturalized in Europe, and occurs in its thousands in at least three bogs in Ireland, several in England, and in Switzerland. It favours extremely swampy conditions, always being at its best in level areas of saturated sphagnum. The purple-veined and often purple-tinted pitchers are slimmer than in the other subspecies, *venosa*, also differing in being shiny and smooth to the touch and in the hood, which does not have a wavy border. The flower is usually slightly smaller, darker red and less subject to variation. There is a rare and attractive naturally occurring form in which all purple coloration is absent, the pitchers being entirely green, and the flowers yellow. The species is found in alkaline bogs in the American Great Lakes region, where it has smaller, more numerous pitchers of brighter colour. Though these have been given a varietal name, var. *riplicola*, by some, its differences appear to be due to its habitat, for in cultivation my own plants soon became indistinguishable from the typical form.

The Southern Pitcher Plant *S. purpurea* ssp. *venosa* occurs in a broken range from a point near New Orleans eastwards along the Gulf Coast and up the eastern coastal plain to New jersey, where it meets and hybridizes with ssp. *purpurea*. I have already mentioned some of its differences from ssp. *purpurea*, and to these one may add that the two projecting lobes on either side of the base of the hood are larger, and only in *venosa* may they be physically brought together to meet, without damaging the pitcher. As well as being wider the pitcher usually has a more highly developed nectar roll around the rim, and the hood is

The Southern Pitcher *S. purpurea* ssp. *venosa* growing on a window-sill

proportionately larger with a characteristic wavy edge. There is great variation in individuals and forms in the coloration of both pitcher and flower. At one end of the extreme you will find pitchers which remain apple-green with a rich network of crimson-maroon veins particularly well marked in the hood and, at the other, forms in which the pitchers darken to such a deep shade of crimson-red that the veins are completely obscured. Similarly, the flowers can be of a beautiful shade of soft pink (epitomized by a Gulf Coast form often termed 'Louis Burke') to deep reddish crimson. There seems a strong case for the selection and naming of a few of the best variants by an official horticultural body.

The Parrot Pitcher plant *S. psittacina* is found in places on the Gulf Coast and also in southern Georgia. Its pitchers form a ground-hugging rosette occasionally reaching a diameter of 30.5cm (12in), although they are more commonly half that

The Hooded Trumpet *S. minor* tricks its victims with the hope of escape through the false 'windows' at the back of the hood

size. They are quite different from those of all other species. Each ends in an inflated structure like a parrot's beak. This is often reddish, and on its back, continuing a little way down the pitcher, white 'windows' are scattered, much as is the Hooded Trumpet.

In the angle between the beak and the top of the pitcher tube is a narrow tunnel-like entrance baited with nectar. Small insects mistaking the windows for exits are most unlikely to relocate this tiny entrance. The rather small flower is

The Parrot Pitcher *S. psittacina*. Under the 'beak' of the large left-hand pitcher is the entry tunnel leading to the translucent false exits

garnet red. The plant grows mainly in low-lying areas subject to periodic flooding, and when submerged the traps catch small water creatures in exactly the same way as a lobster pot does on a large scale. There is a desirable form from the Gulf Coast in which the hood of the pitcher is much more inflated than in the typical form and is better variegated in white and red.

SARRACENIA HYBRIDS

The species readily interbreed, indeed wherever you find two or more growing together in the wild you are likely to find hybrid offspring between them. The fact that species usually flower at slightly different times saves the situation from getting completely out of control. Earlier botanists often mistook these commonly occurring hybrids for species, giving them Latin names, and from this seems to have arisen a curious tradition in which not only were natural interspecific hybrids so named, but so were those produced in horticulture. While in most other plants a named hybrid is normally of one clone (i.e. descended from one seedling), in the case of the Latin-named *Sarracenia* hybrids, the same name is given to seedlings of the same interspecific cross however many times it is repeated. Thus, if you cross *S. flava* with *S. purpurea*, the resulting offspring is always called *S. x catesbaei*. Although these Latin names continue in use, this is a matter of convenience and they are no longer used for modern hybrids. The raiser now usually knows them by their parentages. This may be complicated, in which case he will use a formula or even a number referring to the parentage in his notebook. There is not enough space here to expand upon the recording of pedigrees, formulae and allied technical information, but I have explained these in detail in my earlier book, *Carnivorous Plants*. Very occasionally indeed a hybrid seedling may prove to be of unique horticultural merit, when a clonal name may be justified. In such a case the description, photograph and name should be published in a recognized horticultural journal.

Creating your own hybrids You will find it quite an easy matter and great fun to raise your own hybrids. Certainly, they will take between five and seven years to reach maturity, but watching their stages of growth is exciting, and if you aim to raise new ones yearly you will at length have new mature plants to look forward to each summer. How can you do this? Simply collect some of the freshly released pollen from the floor of the 'umbrella' with a small watercolour brush. This now has to be transferred to the female parts of the flower you wish to pollinate. The structure of the flower is shown on page 46. These are the five stigmas, tiny projections found near the end of the inside surface of each of the five lobes of the umbrella. A few microscopic grains of pollen will stick to each stigma, and each is capable of producing a seed, but I prefer to repeat the process daily while the flowers are in bloom, and in this way more and more seeds will be produced.

Never mix your brushes, or use uncleaned ones which have already been used. This leads to rogue hybrids you did not intend. Also, if you are pollinating, say, *S. purpurea* with *S. rubra* pollen you can also pollinate the *S. rubra* with *S. purpurea* pollen, but to do this you must use separate brushes, or you will obtain at least a large proportion of self-pollinated plants rather than hybrid seed. At petal fall wash the brushes with soap and cold water, rinse well, bring the hairs to a point and dry. Seed does not normally mature before autumn, and is not ripe until the capsule has become dead and brown.

BE METICULOUS

It is always worth being selective in your choice of parent plants. If possible, select plants with individual qualities, such as a finely coloured or shaped pitcher, which you would like transmitted to the offspring. Be meticulous about labelling; a hybrid of unknown origin is of little interest to the professional breeder. Tie an identity label around the flower stem of the seed parent, and make sure that your seed boxes, trays and pots are all clearly labelled. Keep a hybrid record book, giving the progeny of each pollination a number.

This number can be included on each plant label to lessen the risk of confusion. For seed raising, see page 49.

The ease with which the species and hybrids may be cross pollinated means that, as with the rose, the horticultural future of *Sarracenia* lies mainly with hybrids. Though many will be of complex ancestry the professional hybridist will not be so interested in pedigree as in obtaining that single seedling which is of exceptional quality, even if it is a simple interspecific cross. Some fine plants have been raised by a handful of breeders, particularly by Mr Stephen Clemesha of Australia, but for the time of the super plants we must look very much into the future, and I do not think anyone should expect to achieve wonders at their first attempt.

SOME HYBRIDS

Many hundreds of hybrids of different parentages are in cultivation, and here it is only possible to give brief descriptions of the interspecific crosses and of a few others. The cross between *S. flava* and *S. purpurea* is *S. x catesbaei*.

In the wild the *purpurea* parent is always ssp. *venosa*, and this gives wider pitchers than if ssp. *purpurea* is used. In either case they curve upwards and outwards, have a large hood, and are often richly veined. The brick-red flower is large. If *S. x catesbaei* is then crossed back with *S. purpurea* a neat hybrid results, *S. x melanorhoda*. Its pitchers are very similar to its *S. purpurea* parent, but are rather longer and it is often more richly veined and coloured than either parent. If *S. purpurea* (we will assume in all the following cases that we are using ssp. *venosa*) is crossed with *S. oreophila* a strange thing happens. Something very similar to an outsize *S. x catesbaei* results, with a proportionately even larger hood. The upper part of the pitcher and hood are often beautifully tinted a reddish copper. It has no official name, so must go under the label '*S. purpurea x S. oreophila*'. Although a relatively small grower, *S. oreophila* does indeed possess the power of almost invariably lending vigour and size to its hybrid offspring to an extent one does not see in the other species.

When *S. purpurea* is crossed with *S. leucophylla* the resulting seedling is *S. x mitchelliana*, a plant very similar again to *S. x catesbaei*. Differences are that the edge of the hood undulates markedly, the pitcher often becomes strongly suffused with carmine, and there is a strong netted venation of the hood, many of the interspaces often being dappled with whitish-green or pink. The flower is large, dark red and beautiful. The *S. purpurea x S. alata* cross is *S. x exornata*. The coloration of the pitchers is rather lighter than in *S. x catesbaei*, and the flowers are a delicate pink. *S. purpurea x S. rubra* is *S. x chelsonii*, and this will vary a little according to the particular subspecies of *S. rubra* involved, but the pitchers are always narrower than in *S. x catesbaei*, and differ also in being semi-decumbent and more curved, and the hood is narrower. The rube is strongly veined in dark red, and the hood is well netted, while the flower is dark mahogany. The *S. x swaniana*, the *S. purpurea x S. minor* cross has a unique appearance, the pitchers of which are on a constant inwardly inclined curve from their base to the tips of the triangular hood, so that the

S. x excellens 'Lochness' S. leucophylla x S. minor

entire plant can become globe-like when viewed from the side. This is curious rather than beautiful, but the use of a red-pitchered *S. purpurea* in the parentage can result in vividly red-tinted clones which are extremely attractive. The use of *S. purpurea* ssp. *purpurea* in place of ssp. *venosa* in the above crosses will usually result in rather narrower pitchers, and there is sometimes a slight difference in their coloration, but the use of its green-pitchered and yellow-flowered form, ssp. *purpurea heterophylla*, gives hybrids of distinctly individual appearance which are fairly predictable. Crossed with a red-flowered species you can expect to see a hybrid with brick-red to smokey-orange flowers, but the *S. x catesbaei* you will get by crossing it with *S. flava* will differ from the normal one in having yellowish-green pitchers with little or no red veins, and a clear yellow rather than brick-red flower.

A BIZARRE QUALITY

Interspecific hybrids involving the Parrot Pitcher *S. psittacina* are neither functional 'lobster pot' nor pitfall traps. On a single plant one pitcher may attempt to form a hood which never quite fully opens, while another may be more inclined towards the *psittacina* trap. They seem unnatural. All but *S. x courtii* have pitchers which are neither prostrate nor erect, poking outwards at a diversity of angles, which worries me. Nevertheless many collectors do admire them. Certainly the cross with *S. leucophylla*, *S. x wrigleyana*, has in its best forms brilliant coloration, the upper pitcher being white, richly veined in red, and the dark-red flowers are attractive, too. The cross with *S. rubra* is *S. x gilpinii*, with slender, delicately red-veined pitchers and small, dark-red flowers. *S. x Formosa*, the *S. minor* cross, has greenish pitchers with pointed 'beaks' and white variegation with rusty red flowers. Larger and stronger in pitcher, which is usually more 'open', the cross with *S. flava* is certainly grotesque, but has a bizarre quality which you may find attractive. The mahogany-red flowers are quite large. It appears to have no official name, and nor does the *S. alata* cross, which is quite similar but weaker-looking and smaller *S. x courtii*, the *S. purpurea* cross, differs from all the others in its plump, entirely ground-hugging pitchers. These are usually dark-plum red with lighter variegation in the upper part, while the flowers are garnet red.

But it is amongst the upright pitchered hybrids that I find my own favourites, for not only do they inherit an elegance of pitcher lacking in those just described, but these are often beautifully veined, tinted or variegated, while the flowers can be very splendid indeed. Some of the best are of *S. flava* parentage. When this is crossed with *S. alata* the pitcher is not unlike a slender *S. flava*, but with a narrower, more overhanging hood. Mr Stephen Clemesha made the same cross using a red-pitchered form of *S. flava* and a red-throated *S. alata*, the best seedlings of which have resulted in pitchers that become intensely reddish maroon. In both cases the flowers are light yellow. *S. x popei* is the cross with *S. rubra*, and produces pitchers that are typically like those of a small *S. flava* in shape, but each is delicately pencilled in narrow longitudinal maroon veins, which also form a network in the hood. Crossed with *S. minor* we have the hybrid *S. x harperi*, at its best an attractive plant. The pitchers are a bronzy yellowish-green, and slightly maroon veined, the forwardly directed hood is concave in the form of a reversed heart, and the flowers are soft yellow.

The cross with *S. oreophila* would easily be confused with an extra-vigorous *S. flava*, but the older pitchers often acquire a rosy tint, and the phyllodes are similar to those of *S. oreophjila*. The cross with *S. leucophylla* is *S. x moorei*, a plant commonly but incorrectly known as *S. x mooreana*. Its pitchers are pale green with whitish dappling in the hood, while the flowers vary in the seedlings from reddish orange to peach. When using *S. flava* 'Maxima' as one parent, I selected one particularly fine seedling and called its progeny *S. x moorei* 'Marston Clone'. It has all the vigour and size of 'Maxima' both in pitcher and flower, but the flower is a lovely shade of pale orange, reminding one of the harvest moon, while the hood is well mottled in whitish green.

'LOCHNESS'

When crossed with other upright-pitchered species the White Trumpet *S. leucophylla* produces several other attractive hybrids. Of these my favourite is the cross with *S. minor*, *S. x excellens* – excellent indeed! I first made this cross in 1963 and selected the best seedling with brilliant red petals, calling it *S. x* 'Lochness', a name which had to be scrapped when I learned that the cross was already known, named, and occurs in the wild. But since I have seen no other clone of this hybrid, or indeed of any other with such petals, I now know this cultivar as *S. excellens* 'Lochness'.

The concave hood projects almost horizontally forward, and this, together with the entire upper pitcher, is richly variegated with white 'windows' and delicately pencilled with red veins. The flowers are normally any shade from pinkish mahogany to mahogany red. The cross with *S. rubra* is *S. x readii*, alias *S. x farnhamii*. The rather narrow pitchers are maroon-veined and there is whitish variegation on the somewhat *rubra*-like forward-bent hood. The long-stemmed, smallish flowers are blood-red. The cross with *S. alata* produces *S. x areolata*, with slender, pale-green pitchers, a forward-projecting hood which together with the upper pitcher is dappled in lighter variegation, and rusty pink flowers. When crossed with *S. oreophila* a most attractive hybrid results which has not been named. The pitchers are olive green, later bronzy, and the upper part and hood are variegated in whitish-green and veined in maroon, while the flowers are usually of a dusky reddish range.

This brings us to the other interspecific *S. oreophila* hybrids, all of recent horticultural origin and none of which, therefore, have official Latin names. As a result of each cross, one may usually expect hybrids very similar to those you would expect if *S. flava* had been used, except that there is usually greater vigour, and the tell-tale down-turned phyllodes. Thus, *S. oreophila x rubra* is like a strikingly vigorous *S. popei*, while the *x minor* is like a super *S. x harperi*.

Of the remaining interspecific hybrids, *S. x ahlsii* is the *S. rubra x alata* cross, with pitchers akin to an extra large *S. rubra*, though less heavily veined, and with biscuity to plum-red flowers. *S. x rehderi* is the *S. rubra x minor* cross, with pitchers of a bronzy red similar to *S. minor* in form. They are delicately pencilled with maroon longitudinal veins which also form a network in the hood, but the 'windows' of *S. minor* are inherited only as the faintest lighter dappling. The flowers are a combination of plum and biscuit. The *S. alata x minor* cross, which I prefer to know by the non-valid name of *S. x minata*, is somewhat similar in form, but lacks the veins, and has yellow flowers.

Some other Latin names for hybrids are synonyms for interspecific crosses, while others are for some of more complicated parentage. Space will not allow descriptions.

S. x diesneriana is *S. x courtii* crossed with *S. flava*
S. x farnhamii is *S. x readii*
S. x cantabridgiensis is *S. x excellens*
S. x illustrata is *S. alata* by *S. x catesbaei*
S. lushkei is *S. x courtii* by *S. x moorei*
S. x sanderiana is *S. leucophylla* by *S. x readii* and the unspeakable-sounding and
      unspeakable-looking *S. x umlauftiana* is *S. x courtii* by *S. x wrigleyana*
S. x vetteriana is the cross between *S. x illustrata* and *S. x catesbaei*
S. x vittata maculata is the cross between *S. purpurea* and *S. x chelsonii*
S. x vogeliana is *S. x courtii* by *S. x catesbaei*
S. x willmottae is *S. x catesbaei* by *S. purpurea*

Which, in alphabetical order, brings me to the excellent but problematical *S. x willissii*. The plant generally known under this name has a pitcher of very similar form in trumpet and hood to that of *S. x mitchelliana*, but differs considerably from that plant in coloration. The young pitcher soon becomes tinted with coral pink, later deepening to pinkish red in the upper pitcher and hood, and there is not a hint of the whitish dappling, inherited from *S. leucophylla*, seen in the hood of *S. x mitchelliana*. Though its origin and parentage remain a mystery, I strongly suspect *S. leucophylla* and *S. purpurea venosa* influence here.

This is a splendid plant with large, deep-red flowers, especially valuable in breeding, for its seedlings frequently inherit the bright coral-pink pitcher coloration. But in Veitch's original account he states its parentage to be *S. x courtii x S. x melanorhoda*. Such a plant could only have squat pitchers of very different appearance. Could he have been mistaken? Could there have been a muddle in the pollen used, or in the recording of the pollination, or is it simply that we have the wrong plant? If Veitch's account of its parentage is accepted in horticulture, numerous hybrid pedigrees must be thrown into confusion. For this reason my advice to anyone making or having the *S. x courtii x S. x melanorhoda* cross is never to attach the name *S. willissii* to it.

The Cobra Lily: Darlingtonia

The Cobra Lily's flowers have curious 'bites' in the petals; these are the holes which pollinating insects go through

Bearing an uncanny likeness to a cobra poised to strike, this is surely the strangest looking of all the pitcher plants. Yet this is not a case of plant mimicry – the similarity is purely accidental, and the cobra's hood and forked tongue are essential parts of an elaborate trap.

There is only one species, *D. californica*, a native of the mountains of northern California and Oregon. Nectar glands occur all over the outside of the pitcher, but the forked 'tongue' is extra-heavily baited with these and leads directly to further rich supplies around the small circular mouth situated just under the inflated dome or 'head'. The roof of the dome is lit by a mosaic of completely transparent 'windows' mullioned with green or reddish veins, and insects enter the pitcher mistaking the windowed area for an exit, in much the same way as in the Hooded Pitcher Plant, and become victims by the same method. But there is a difference, for strangely this species does not secrete its own digestive juices. Instead, it secretes pure water within the pitcher which forms a bath in the lower part of the tube. This is the medium in which bacteria break up the soft parts of the insects, and the nutrients thus released into solution are absorbed into the plant. The pitcher is curiously twisted in a spiral along its length, thus allowing its front to face outwards. The wing forms a ramp from ground level to the mouth, and proves a popular path for ants.

In its native mountains it is often found in large colonies alongside streams and around springheads. In high altitudes it is often covered by snow in the winter, but it is also found almost down to sea level where it is extremely hot in summer. However, in the latter case the roots are always kept cool by cold water which has recently emerged from the ground, and this provides the main key to its cultivation, as explained below.

In my experience this plant only thrives when it is growing in pure live sphagnum moss. The plant's roots require plenty of room, for from the main rhizome the mature plant sends out other mini-rhizomes, or stolons, which travel considerable distances, often circling the inside of the pot several times before surfacing to form a new young plant, and these should not be cramped. A plant 10–20cm (4–8in) high will do well in a 20cm (8in) pot, but an ideal container for a larger plant is either a plastic cat-litter box or washing-up bowl with adequate drainage holes drilled in the bottom. You might want to choose an agreeable colour, such as dark green, dark brown or black, preferably matching that of your other pots. If you find it impossible to obtain live sphagnum, a compost of 1 part

The 'head' of the Cobra Lily, showing the forked 'tongue', the mouth and the windowed dome. The curious twisting of the pitcher is also obvious

orchid bark, 1 part moss peat, and 1 part horticultural Perlite is the only alternative to consider using. Watering is the most vital consideration. Stand the pots and container permanently in the water tray in the coolhouse, but this in itself is not sufficient. The root system in nature is used to constant movement of cool water, and to imitate this, also water regularly from above. In winter it is sufficient to do this once a week, but in summer I like to do it once a day at least – twice if possible when the weather is hot. If this is not done the root system will often collapse, resulting in the death of a plant. Apply sufficient soft water with the sprinkler to flush through – say, 275ml (half a pint) of water per 20cm (8in) pot. I cannot explain why this system is successful. Perhaps it helps to keep the root system cool, but as the cooler conditions can only last for a limited time I fancy that it could discourage the build-up of potentially harmful micro-organisms (generating heat during their metabolism) around the root system. The point is that it works!

The maturity (that is to say, the ability to produce flowers) of the Cobra Lily has even less connection with size of pitcher than it does in the other American

Pitcher plants. Indeed, flowers are often produced by plants with pitchers no taller than 10cm (4in). Yet curiously the size of pitcher will tend to increase annually for many years to over 60cm (24in) high, yet pitchers nearly twice as high are to be found in the wild.

Propagation The best way is by the careful detachment of stolons bearing small but well-formed young plants. If the plant is growing in a suitably wide container, such as an adapted basin or deep tray, this can usually be done with very little disturbance to the mother plant. Propagation by division of the plant itself is not recommended unless the clump has become very wide and thick, for root disturbance of this kind can retard growth for a long period. There is no need to divide thick clumps as in *Sarracenia*, and indeed the Cobra Lily very rarely contracts *Botrytis* when in a clump, and seems then at its best. Hand pollination is usually necessary to produce seed in any quantity, but seed seldom germinates well, and the seedlings may take ten years to reach maturity. Germination is extremely irregular, some seeds taking six weeks while others may take months to do so. Raise them as advised for *Sarracenia* and only transfer them to pure sphagnum when the pitchers are about 5cm (2in) long.

As might be expected of mountain plants, the Cobra Lily is hardy and makes an ideal subject for the artificial peat bog in temperate regions.

Pests and diseases are even less inclined to strike than in *Sarracenia*, but where these occur they are of the same kinds and should be treated by the methods recommended on pages 50 and 51.

The South American Sun Pitchers: Heliamphora

THE PITCHER PLANTS OF NORTH AND SOUTH AMERICA

All these pitcher plants have trumpet-shaped leaves which are traps baited with nectar to attract nectar-feeding insects. Victims falter on the slippery surface and fall to the bottom of the pitcher tube where they die and are digested. These plants have no moving parts – they do not need them because they are some of the most efficient traps in nature. All this they have in common but they differ from one another in structure, appearance and technique.

The sun pitchers are natives of those strange, almost vertically-sided table mountains which occur like widely scattered islands on the Sierra Paceraima highlands within and adjoining southern Venezuela. Here they live in relatively cool conditions in marked contrast to those found in the sweltering rainforests beneath. Isolated by both climate and distance, different species have evolved on separate table mountains, each of the known six species of sun pitcher coming from its own individual one, and as this is a very imperfectly explored and botanised part of the world I suspect that yet more may be found on others. These plants bear the most primitive of pitchers, even though they are cousins of the more sophisticated plants we have already considered.

The pitcher may appear to be little more than a rolled leaf, though examination shows that it is much more complex than that. However, it does lack many of the finer details of design we see in the other genera, and it very much tallies with my idea of what we might have expected to see in the more remote ancestors of the pitcher plants of today. Rain collects in the pitcher as far as the slit, a little distance below the expanding 'bell' – or the drainage hole beneath it – present in some species. Nectar glands are scattered about on the outside of the pitcher and more heavily within the bell. The foothold offered by the latter and on the surface below is very uncertain, so that feeding insects tend to be jettisoned into the rainwater beneath. Here digestion is completed entirely by bacteria, because there are no digestive glands.

But what of the more sophisticated mechanism? The bell tapers at the top, back to a narrow stalk which is inclined forward and bears a downward-facing spoon-like object called the nectar spoon. Its interior is liberally studded with nectar glands so large that they can easily be seen with the naked eye. Too little attention has been given to this structure, which seems to me to have at least three useful functions other than the obvious one of simply providing extra bait. The frequent rains typical of these mountains will cause the nectar in the bell to be as frequently washed away, and with it its attraction for nectar-feeders. But the canopy formed by the nectar spoon perfectly protects the nectar beneath it from the rain, so that the spoon remains an attractive bait at all times.

Secondly, winged insects tend to find the shelter of foliage during rain, and will not remain upon the exposed surface of the open bell at such a time. But the spoon provides an insect with shelter, and it therefore remains constantly at risk of becoming a victim of the pitcher. The size of the spoon is not large; it will not, for example, usually accommodate more than one housefly-size insect at a time, and this might be thought to be a disadvantage. I was inclined to think this myself until observing a plant which I had placed upon my garden table. A fly alighted on the bell and walked up to the nectar spoon, where it remained feeding. This was followed by another of the same species and size which proceeded to walk to the spoon, where there was not enough room for the two. A jostle for space followed, with the inevitable result that one lost its footing on the uncertain surface.

The pitchers of all six species are perhaps more curious than beautiful, but the several nodding lily-like flowers on tall, usually reddish scapes are very lovely, as you will see in the photograph. These may be white, usually turning to pale pink, or soft pink on opening. They are produced at all times of year, providing a welcome sight in winter.

Cultivation This is not particularly difficult, but as propagation using present methods is a slow affair they are likely to remain rare in cultivation, and expensive where offered for sale. This could change if a satisfactory method of tissue culture is found.

I favour a compost consisting of equal parts of pure live sphagnum moss and horticultural Perlite, and a 13–15cm (5–6in) pot. Both pitchers and roots are unusually brittle, and when planting one should ensure that the latter are snugly firm without using the kind of pressure which might break them. The rhizome itself should be just beneath the surface. After planting, apply soft water gently with the sprinkler to settle in the roots. Water by the tray system, but also water the pot from the top daily during the summer only. Always spray the foliage with soft water at least once daily, both summer and winter, but if possible several times a day in summer. Kenneth Burras, the quality of whose *Heliamphora nutans* at the Oxford Botanic Gardens is famous, set up an excellent system. Every student or employee who entered the *Heliamphora* house was asked to spray the plants each time. The spray is a substitute for the rainy conditions in the wild, and it also ensures that there is always water in the pitchers. They appreciate sun, even though they do not see much of it in the wild, but light shading must be applied to the glass in late spring and must not be removed until the autumn.

Unlike *Sarracenia* and *Darlingtonia* this is not a good insect-catcher under glass, even though it proves to be efficient enough when temporarily placed out of doors – a risk that I do not recommend your taking. But it benefits from foliar feed applied as a spray to the foliage only. Spray twice weekly in summer with 'Orchidquick' at the rate given under *Nepenthes* (see page 123). An alternative recommended by Joseph Mazrimas is the slow-release pelleted fertilizer Osmocote 14-14-14. He uses a measure containing 3.5ml per pot, feeding in March and August only.

Normal coolhouse temperatures are satisfactory providing they do not fall below a winter minimum of 5.5°C (42°F), and it is advisable to try to avoid temperatures of over 25.5°C (78°F) in summer.

The beautiful flowers of the sun pitcher
H. nutans

Sun pitcher *H. nutans*

Propagation Seed, unfortunately, is seldom produced and hard to come by, but if available can be raised as recommended for *Sarracenia*. At the time of writing propagation is almost invariably carried out by division. This can only be done when the plant has formed a good-sized clump with at least five crowns, and it must then be carried out with extreme care, remembering the extremely brittle nature of the entire plant. Carefully knock it out of its pot, and place the roots with all the compost intact in a bowl or bucket of water. The compost can now be gently teased away, leaving all the roots unbroken. Once this is removed you will get a clear picture of what material can be used for propagation. Select only those rhizome branches which have at least one good head of pitchers and some roots attached, remove with a sharp knife, and pot up as previously directed.

Should you accidentally break the roots, treat the rhizome as a cutting, potting it but placing it under a propagating dome. Place it in a good light, but protected

Heliamphora minor

from direct sun. After six weeks it should have rooted, and a little air should be admitted by propping one side of the propagator cover on a small object, allowing more air in after a week. Remove the propagator the following week.

Pest and diseases These plants are not particularly prone to pests, but when they strike they can be treated by the same methods recommended for those of *Sarracenia*. Scale insects are occasionally troublesome. The plants do not seem particularly susceptible to fungal attack, though you can give them an occasional light spray with Benomyl when carrying out routine spraying of *Sarracenia* in winter. Here be warned – copper-based fungicides are deadly to *Heliamphora*! I lost all my *H. heterodoxa* and *H. minor* stock through using such a spray a few years ago. If you use sprays other than those specifically mentioned under *Sarracenia*, it is a good idea to experiment first on a guinea-pig plant, if you can spare it.

THE SPECIES

H. nutans is at present the most common species in cultivation, and comes from Mount Duida, the 'Lost World' of Conan Doyle's novel. Similar, though more attractive in pitcher, is *H. heterodoxa*, with pitchers that grow to about 25cm (10in), and one of the largest nectar spoons in the genus. It is a native of Mount Ptari-Tepui. The smallest is *H. minor*, from Mount Auyan-Tepui, in which the pitchers seldom exceed 7.5cm (3in) in length. Its nectar spoon is the smallest of any, and seldom develops at all in cultivated plants. *H. neblinae* is found on the Cerro de la Neblina. It has a long, rather narrow bell, and in proportion to the pitcher size the nectar spoon is the largest of any species. There are three distinct varieties. *H. neblinae* var. *neblinae* has been recently introduced to cultivation and has white flowers; white petal-like sepals tipped red, and shorter pitchers. Neither of these varieties is yet in cultivation.

H. ionasi, occurring naturally on Mount Ilu-Tepui, is a species of quite outstanding interest. This produces gigantic rosettes of the largest pitchers in the genus. Up to 46cm (18in) high, it is of unusual form, being widely flared at the mouth, like a French Horn, and surmounted by a large nectar spoon. It usually becomes nicely suffused with red with age.

H. tatei differs from all others in forming shrubby stems to 1.5m (5ft) on open savannahs, while it can scramble to a height of 4m (13ft) in light woodland. Its pitchers are narrow and long, the bell is tubular, flaring only towards the top, and the rise in gradient of its edge from front to back is not great. The nectar spoon is wide-stalked and rather large. Of the two varieties, *H. tatei* var. *tatei* is the typical form (the former *H. tyleri* now being considered identical to it), and var. *macdonaldiae* differs only in that the inner surface of its bell is nearly hairless.

The Portuguese Sundew: Drosophyllum

The Portuguese Sundew in flower

A group of unrelated genera use one of the very simplest methods in overcoming their prey. Alighting creatures caught by sticky mucilage secreted by numerous glands, are overwhelmed and suffocated by this, and then digested by a secondary secretion of enzymes and acid. No plant movements are used at any stage in the process, and the plants have been aptly described by F.E. Lloyd as 'passive flypapers'.

The only species, *D. lusitanicum*, is a native of dry coastal hillsides in Spain, Portugal and Morocco. The light green, semi-upright foliage is up to 20cm (8in) long, very narrow and tapering to a point. They rather resemble in shape and arrangement enormous pine needles, and indeed the plant is known as the 'Dewy Pine' in Portugal. The semi-upright stance of the foliage exposes the underside of the leaf to view and to the alighting insect, and it is this side which bears the red mucilage-secreting glands. These are borne on short stalks and each has a large glittering drop of clear colourless fluid. This is not as tenacious as in other sticky-leaved carnivorous plants, for the technique used by this species in overcoming its prey is rather different.

THE STATIC GLUEY TRAPS

The struggling insect is usually able to break free from the glands on which it first alights, but in doing so the fluid breaks away with it, adhering to its body. The process is repeated as it advances down the leaf, until the build-up of mucilage over its body smothers it. At this stage the microscopic glands on the leaf surface underneath the insect secrete digestive juices, and absorb the resulting nutrients. After the foliage dies it persists on the plant. The resulting grey skirts of old leaves set off the live heads well, and if it is removed this only results in a very straggly-looking plant. In the spring each head produces a fine show of large, bright-yellow flowers, each one about 2.5cm (1in) across. These are soon followed by seed heads consisting of a strange, almost transparent capsule which splits to release rather large, black, pear-shaped seeds.

Cultivation This was once looked upon as a difficult plant, but it is simple enough to grow once you know how. It is most unusual among carnivorous plants in favouring dry conditions in the wild, so it is not surprising that a wet collar, poor drainage (especially in winter) and misting or spraying of the foliage will all rapidly kill it. It also hates root disturbance. The following method overcomes all such risks and if strictly followed your plants should survive without trouble for ten to fifteen years, at least.

This plant is remarkable as it detests being moved about in such a way that stress is caused to the trunk. Never buy it as a growing plant, for the movements involved are, ultimately, likely to kill it. This is a plant always to be grown from seed, obtainable from carnivorous plant specialists, and a large plant may thus be raised within one year. You will also need one or more 11cm (4.3in) clay pot, and one 20cm (8in), clay pot. These must be of clay, since non-porous pots will not lend themselves to the method. You will also need some sphagnum moss (it need

The Portuguese Sundew *D. lusitanicum*.
The young leaves unfurl from a coil
facing outwards

not be live), moss peat, horticultural sand, John Innes Compost No.2 (in countries
where this is not available I am sure a good loam-based potting compost would
do), and some crocks of broken clay pot.

Take the 11cm (4.5in) pot and insert through the drainage hole a wick
consisting of a few strands of the sphagnum (see overleaf). Put one or two large
drainage crocks over the moss, concave side down-facing, and make sure the wick
protrudes internally so that it will be in full contact with part of the thin layer of
sphagnum – now cover the crocks with the thin layer of sphagnum.

Fill the pot to within 6mm (0.25in) of the top with a well mixed compost of 2
parts peat, 2 parts potting soil, and 1.5 parts sand. Gently firm this, and now sow
three seeds in the central area, about 2cm (0.78in) apart and 5mm (0.19in) deep.

Gently firm. Place the pot in 2cm (0.78in) of water until the surface appears damp, remove to drain and then place an upside-down saucer over the pot to check evaporation and cut out the light. There will be some evaporation from the sides of the pot, of course, so another watering by immersion may be necessary before germination, and you much check that the compost never becomes dry.

Examine regularly, and you will usually find that the first seed germinates in three to six weeks' time. Immediately remove the saucer, place the pot in a sunny position, and water by brief immersion as before whenever the compost appears dryish, never allowing it to become dry. Never apply water to the top. A little time after all the seedlings have germinated, carefully remove the weaker two so as not to disturb the stronger one, the object of sowing three seeds having been to ensure that one at least will germinate, and that this may be a strong grower. Keep your plant growing like this until it is in its eighth leaf.

Take the larger pot, put a few large crocks over the drainage holes, concave side down-facing, cover these with a thin layer of sphagnum, and then half fill it with a compost mixed exactly as before, firming this. Now place the smaller pot in

Stages in propogating *Drosophyllum* by seed

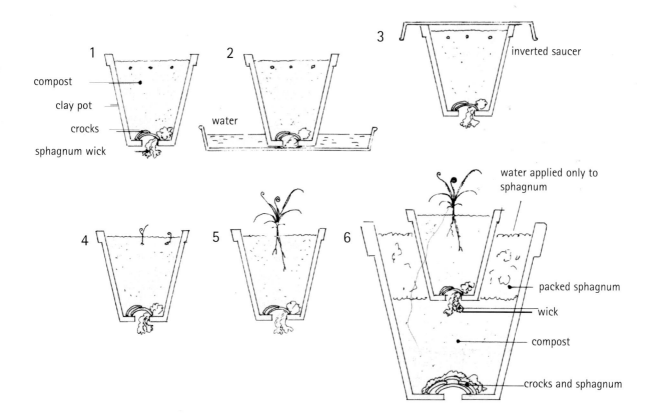

the centre (see diagram), and if its top is not well above the rim of the larger pot you will need to add more compost to the larger pot to ensure that it is. Make sure that the sphagnum wick in the drainage hole of the smaller pot is extended so that it is in full contact with the compost in the larger pot. Now fill the gap between the sides of the two pots with sphagnum, lightly firming this. Place the pot in a sunny position close to the glass.

From this moment water the sphagnum in the larger pot, which acts as a reservoir. The inner pot absorbs its requirements from the sphagnum via its absorbent clay sides. The top of the compost in the inner pot will always remain fairly dry. Water the sphagnum via its absorbent clay sides. Water the sphagnum fairly frequently in summer, keeping the moss rather moist always, but in winter wait until the moss is dryish without having become crisp before watering.

The plant must never be repotted or have its roots disturbed in any way, for either will cause inevitable death. There is ample room for many years of growth, for the roots will enter the compost in the larger pot through the drainage hole in the smaller one, and will find enough space there.

The Rainbow Plant: Byblis

The flowers of the Giant Rainbow *Byblis gigantea*

The two species in this Australian genus differ greatly in size, but both bear long, narrow leaves, each of which terminates in a point which on close examination is seen to be a tiny knob. These leaves are held at an acute angle to the stem. Though the entire leaf surface and stems are covered in tiny sticky glands it is, as in the Dewy Pine, only the lower leaf surface which is involved with catching and devouring prey. Here the mucilage-secreting glands are held on long, narrow stalks and bear drops of a strong 'glue' capable of retaining comparatively large insects. As in the Dewy Pine, digestion is carried out by other microscopic glands which secrete the digestive juices and absorb the products of digestion. The flowers of both species are beautiful. They are five-petalled, held on a long, rather narrow stem arising from a leaf axil, and borne profusely and continuously throughout the summer.

The Giant Rainbow *B. gigantea* from Western Australia is by far the larger of the two, producing annual stems which reach a height of 61cm (24in) in the wild. The leaves are a yellowish green and are up to 30cm (12in) long, while the petals are rich lilac-pink to lilac-purple, with bright yellow stamens. The Lesser Rainbow Plant *Byblis liniflora* is an exceptionally pretty little annual, from 10–28cm (4–11in) in height. Seen in a group, the numerous glittering glands seem to impart a magical quality which one could liken to a radiant mist, and upon this the delicate rosy lilac flowers seem to float. It occurs in the north of Western Australia, as well as in Queensland.

Pests and diseases I have neither experienced nor heard of either species suffering from any pest or disease in cultivation.

Cultivation Each requires different treatment. *B. gigantean* should be planted in a 15cm (6in) full-length plastic pot in a mixture of equal parts horticultural sand and moss peat. Stand this in a saucer in a sunny position in the cool greenhouse close to the glass.

In summer put sufficient soft water in the saucer for the pot to not quite suck up, replenishing this when it is empty. In winter aim to keep the compost moist rather than wet, but the saucer mainly empty. In cultivation the annual stems may persist for much longer than they would in nature, but when they become yellowish and new green growth is seen to be appearing towards their bases or elsewhere, they should be pruned away. For *B. liniflora*, see the section on propagation overleaf.

Propagation and cultivation of *B. liniflora* is an easy matter. The plants produce abundant viable seed without the need for hand pollination. This should be sown annually, in late winter or early spring, sparingly on the surface of a 50:50 mix of horticultural sand and moss peat in a 12.5cm (5in) dwarf pot or deep seed tray. It likes a sunny position in the coolhouse. This plant comes from wet places, so water on the tray system with soft water.

B. gigantean can be propagated by stem and root cuttings and also from seed. Stem cuttings rarely fail. They should be taken in early July, making a straight cut across the stem just beneath a leaf base, about 4–5cm (1.5–2in) from the tip of the shoot. Remove the leaves from the bottom 25mm (1in) or so of the cutting together with flower and flower-bud stalks, using a fine pair of scissors. Put the cuttings aside for about ten minutes, and meanwhile take a 15cm (6in) plastic pot and fill with the mixture given above. Dip the tips of the cuttings in rooting powder and plant firmly to about one-third the depth of the cutting. Place the pot in a saucer of soft water until the surface is seen to be moist, remove, and place the pot in a light place which is entirely protected from direct sunlight. Cover with a propagator cover.

After six weeks or so, clear signs of growth should be evident. At this stage gradually introduce more air to the propagator by tilting the cover a little more each day, removing it after ten days, but do not introduce to direct sunlight for another ten days. A single cutting may be allowed to grow on in the same pot, but if there are more than one you should pot them about four weeks after this time.

CUTTINGS

Root cuttings may be taken from large, well-established plants only, in mid spring. Knock the plant out of its pot and immerse the roots in a bucket of water, gently teasing away the compost from the roots so that they remain uninjured. Try to select enough of the fattest roots for your requirements, while still leaving an adequate root system for the mother plant. Make clean cuts with a sharp knife, cutting the selected roots into lengths 2.5–3cm (1–1.2in) long. Fill a 12.5cm (5in) pot with the specified compost, firming and levelling it so that it is about 6mm (0.25in) short of the brim. Lay the root cuttings flat on the surface, covering with no more than 3mm (0.12in) of the same compost. Place the pot in a saucer of soft water until the surface of the compost is moist, remove and place in a shaded place, preferably under a propagator cover to conserve moisture. The first growth may appear within six weeks, but can take considerably longer. At this stage remove the cover and treat as recommended for the mature plant. The young plants may be potted as soon as it appears that no more will emerge.

B. gigantean may also be raised from seed. This never seems to germinate unless exposed to fire, and it appears that bush fires activate it into growth in the wild. In order to emulate this, take a fire-proof (i.e. clay) 12.5cm (5in) dwarf pot, fill with the compost previously mentioned, and firm level with the brim. Scatter the seed over the surface and do not cover it. Pile short pieces of dry hay to form a loose mound over this, and ignite it from the bottom, ensuring that it burns down to ground level. Lightly water the compost from above with the sprinkler when it has cooled, so as to release chemicals produced by the burning into the compost surface. Stand the pot in a shallow saucer of soft water until the seedlings appear, afterwards treating these as for the parent plant.

This plant does not normally set seed in cultivation, for the pollen is not released by the anthers. This only occurs in nature when it is triggered by the vibrating wings of certain moth pollinators. In cultivation, this action can be simulated with the aid of any tuning fork, surprisingly enough. Strike the tuning fork, touch the anthers, and the pollen is released in a cloud which can be collected on a small watercolour brush held in front of them as this is done. Transfer this to the stigma of another flower, and repeat the process from flower to flower.

The Lesser Rainbow *B. liniflora.* Its fragile delicacy does not prevent it from being an efficient trap: this one has caught a mosquito

Triphyophyllum

This plant differs from other carnivorous species in three respects. The carnivorous habit is a short phase only in the life history of the plant, and it has three different kinds of adult leaf, only one of which is carnivorous. There is only one species in its genus, *T. peltatum*. Although first attempts at its cultivation were not successful, this is often the case with a newly introduced plant and should not be difficult in the stovehouse. Although I cannot, therefore, give details of cultivation, nonetheless I feel that this book would be incomplete without a brief reference to this 'passive flypaper'.

The seedling first forms a stem to about 92cm (36in), when its growth temporarily ceases. This often has a head of sword-shaped leaves about 36cm (14in) long, giving the impression of a small palm tree. Suddenly several long, wire-like, nearly upright leaves uncoil from the centre. These are carnivorous, and bear stalked mucilage-secreting glands of two sizes. Insects caught on these are soon swamped by further secretion from the glands with which they have made contact, and the secretion contains enzymes which digest the soft parts of their bodies.

After two or three years a bud in the centre develops into a shoot. This is clothed with alternately arranged lance-shaped leaves, each ending in a pair of hooks which enable the vine to climb into the tree tops. Here small scented white flowers are produced, followed by fruiting bodies from which hang curiously winged seeds. The wing is in the form of a flat and perfectly circular discus, up to about 10cm (4in) in diameter, and pink to red in colour, the seed being implanted in its centre. Once detached, the discus glides away, and may carry seed for a considerable distance.

Above: Winged seeds and developing fruit

Below: Carnivorous and non-carnivorous leaves of *Triphyophyllum*

The Butterworts: Pinguicula

This is surely the most uncarnivorous-looking of all the carnivorous genera. The butterworts produce usually flat and almost invariably neat rosettes of foliage. The leaves themselves may hardly look sticky, but on touching them you will find that they have a distinctly buttery feel, which, on closer examination, proves to be due to the secretion of almost microscopic stalked glands covering the upper leaf surface in their tens of thousands. On alighting, small insects stick to this, are overwhelmed and digested in a way very similar to the Rainbow Plant *Byblis*. In most species the flat leaf blade, and the usually upturned rolled edges, are capable of movement. This is very gradual, and so cannot normally help catching prey. Its main advantage is in improving the efficiency of digestion: the leaf edge will often enfold the victim's body, and thus put more digestive leaf surface in contact with it, while the main part of the blade will become cupped under the prey, forming a saucer in which digestive fluid can be held. In areas of high rainfall, the ability of the edges to roll over prey undoubtedly has the added advantage of protecting it from being washed away by the rain before it can be absorbed.

The flowers are two-lipped and spurred, the upper lip has two lobes, the lower normally three. At one extreme the flower may be wide and trumpet-shaped, as in most European species, and at the other very narrow, as in the Mexican *P. moranensis*. Almost all the species are highly attractive, some being delicately pretty, while many possess real beauty in varying degrees. A number are indeed so ravishingly lovely that they may be compared with the finest orchids. Yet it is only comparatively recently that the great horticultural value of these plants has begun to be recognized. For convenience the species are divided into several groups on a horticultural, rather than botanical, basis.

SPECIES FORMING WINTER BUDS

Many species from cooler climates, and virtually all those from central and northern Europe, die back to tight 'resting buds' of green leaf scales in winter. Usually rootless and unattached, the clumps are then easily spread about by the elements, aiding their distribution. These buds are often referred to as hibernacula (sing. hibernaculum). In addition they also produce 'gemmae'. A gemma is, in effect, a miniature resting bud, attached often in great numbers around the base of a resting bud. Those gemmae that break off are often fully capable of producing a mature plant within one growing season, and may provide the best means of propagation when a large stock is required.

General cultivation With the exception of *P. vallisneriifolia*, all these species require cool conditions. In cooler temperate regions, use the coldframe method explained on page 17. In warmer conditions they cannot properly build up a winter resting bud, which leads to their death. So, if you live in a warmer climate it will be necessary to grow them under specially controlled conditions, such as a terrarium or growing room, with an air conditioner to control temperature, and fluorescent lighting giving a twelve-hour photoperiod in spring, gradually rising to sixteen hours at midsummer, and declining to twelve hours again by autumn. In winter it is not necessary to use such a unit, as the loose hibernacula and gemmae can be put in polythene bags and stored in the main (not freezing) compartment of your fridge. An exception is *P. alpina*, because it retains its roots; but in this case the entire potted plant may be placed there. While they like plenty of light, you should shade them from direct sunlight, especially in the middle of the day. Compost requirements vary, and are given under the species. The treatment for *P. vallisneriifolia* varies only in that it must be grown in coolhouse conditions.

Propagation This is easily done by division of the resting buds in the spring, before they come into growth. Press these into the compost, so that the base third only is below ground level. Alternatively, gemmae may be used, and often vast numbers of new plants may be raised where these have been produced in quantity. They will be found around the base of the parent hibernaculum, and should be just spaced about 2.5cm (1in) apart on the surface of the compost, in dwarf pots or deep polythene seed trays, and otherwise treated as the parent plants.

Seed is a slower method, but is the best for *P. alpina* and *P. vulgaris* and its forms, and can be the method of obtaining some species. Seed is not long-lived, so should always have been freshly collected the previous summer. The flowers are seldom self-pollinating, so if you want to set your own seed (there is often a scarcity of pollinating insects) it is wise to pollinate your own. To do this use a tiny watercolour brush with only a few hairs. Carefully thrust this up the tube of a flower once, and it will collect an often minute, unnoticeable but sufficient amount of pollen. If you have only one flower, a second thrust up the tube after removal will self-pollinate it, but if you have a second flower of the same species it should be inserted into this one to ensure vigorous offspring, and the brush may then be used to pollinate the first flower with the pollen thus obtained from the second. To be sure of a successful 'set' you may repeat the process daily.

Sow about three weeks after mid-winter on the compost surface in dwarf pots or plastic seed boxes, using the same compost recommended for the mature species, and water on the tray system. Do not cover the seed. In cool climates keep in the coldframe as described, ventilating well. To ensure good germination the seed should be frosted several times, so remove the pots or trays on at least three frosty nights, standing them in a suitably exposed place, and returning them to the frame the following morning. In frost-free areas an alternative would be to

The large-flowered Butterwort
P. grandiflora produces an abundance of
violet flowers in the typical form

place them in the freezer three or more times. Good germination usually follows in the spring, but for some unaccountable reason some seed waits a further year. In such cases you should subject the container to frost again at the same time the following winter, keeping it moist (using the tray system) and shaded. Prick out the seedlings into pots and boxes as soon as they are large enough to handle. They usually reach adult size within sixteen months of germination.

Pests and diseases These are mainly slugs, snails and woodlice. Attacks from all may be minimized if you stand the pots away from the sides of the water tray, thus not allowing the pests access. Leatherjackets, too, can be a problem, and very occasionally the plants may be attacked by aphids on the unsticky undersides of the leaves. Control these as recommended under *Sarracenia*, but it helps to include a small quantity of a suitable soil pesticide in the compost mixture. To calculate the quantity required, estimate the number of pots full that you have mixed, and add sufficient scatterings to the pesticide for that number of posts.

THE SPECIES

The Common Butterwort *P. vulgaris* is widely distributed on the hills, mountains and moors of North America, Siberia and Europe, including Britain, growing in alkaline as well as acid conditions. It is an elegant plant with yellowish-green, narrowly oblong leaves with conspicuously rolled edges, in flat rosettes up to about 13cm (5in) in diameter. It is especially noticeable when colonies are seen clinging like starfishes in fissures of wet rocks, the leaves tightly pressed to their contours. Each scape bears a single violet flower 22mm (0.86in) long, with a white spot in its funnel-shaped mouth.

In addition to colour variants distinct geographic forms occur. Of these, *f. alpicola* has flowers twice as large as the type in *f. albida*, which are almost white, while in *f. bicolour* they are violet and white. Use a compost of 3 parts moss peat to 1 part sand, and a 12.5cm (5in) dwarf pot. Mound the surface a little, and embed a few small pieces of rock in the surface to keep the roots cool. Up to five resting buds may then be inserted in the fissures between.

Of species closely related to the above, *P. macroceras* is found in Northern America, Russia and Japan, and has a larger lower lip and longer spur, while *P. balcanica* from the Dinaric and Pindus ranges is a large-flowered form.

The Large-Flowered or Irish Butterwort *P. grandiflora* is surely the most beautiful of all European species when in flower. The oblong to oval yellowish-green leaves are in rosettes up to 15.5cm (6in) across. The flowers in its typical form are up to 3cm (1.2in) long, of rich violet with darker veins and a white throat. It occurs in hills and mountains in Ireland, France, Switzerland, Andorra and Spain. The lovely form *pallida* from the Western Jura has similar but pale lilac-blue flowers, with a violet ring around the white, violet-veined throat. In Andorra, not far from Soldeu, I came across almost every colour graduation from a beautiful lilac-pink through pale violet to the typical deep form, and it is clear to me that the colour range of this species in cultivation could be greatly extended. The subspecies *rosea* is found only in the mountains near Grenoble, and has large soft-rose flowers. For all, I recommend a compost of 4 parts moss peat, 2 parts John Innes No. 2, 1 part sand, with some rocks on the surface as recommended for *P. vulgaris*. Best propagated from its vast production of gemmae, or seed.

The Long-Leaved Butterwort *P. longifolia* of the Pyrenees has spidery leaves about the same size but very narrow and lance-shaped, the upturned edges kinked here and there; the total effect is spidery. The flowers, too, are similar but of a paler violet with a large white patch in the throat; the lower lip is covered with white hair, and the spur is longer. Of its two subspecies, ssp. *caussensis* has a much paler flower, and ssp. *reichenbachiana* is smaller in both foliage and flower.

The Pale Butterwort *P. lusitanicum* growing on Dartmoor, England

Cultivate as for *P. grandiflora*, but include a teaspoonful of crushed chalk to each potful of compost when mixing.

P. Corsica is very similar to *P. grandiflora*, but my form has beautiful palest-violet flowers with deep-violet veins in the throat and on the outside of the tube and spur, and looks well when intermixed with that species. It comes from Corsica. From the European Alps comes the Southern Butterwort *P. leptoceras*, which in

Hand pollinate the rarity *P. hirtiflora*

appearance is somewhere between *P. vulgaris* and *P. grandiflora*, though weaker-looking and inferior to both. The flowers are paler, and have a large white hairy area on the lower lip. Treat as for *P. x scullyi*, the hybrid between *P. vulgaris* and *P. grandiflora*, which often occurs naturally where the two species meet. It can be attractive, and is best treated as for *P. grandiflora*.

The Alpine Butterwort *P. alpina* is found in most of the European mountains, has been found again in Scotland where it was thought to be extinct, and descends to sea level in Scandinavia. The somewhat triangular leaves are in a rosette seldom exceeding 5cm (2in) in diameter, while the white flowers with orange to yellow throats are variable, but most attractive in the best forms. The roots do not die away in winter in this species, and it hates root disturbance at all times. Therefore always raise your plants from seed, transplanting them when large enough to handle and keeping them permanently in the same pots afterwards. I use a 12.5cm (5in) dwarf pot and a compost of 3 parts moss peat, 1 part John Innes No. 2, and 2 parts sand, embedding a few pieces of magnesium limestone tufa rock in the surface.

The Arctic Butterwort *P. villosa* is a perfect miniature from the arctic and subarctic regions of North America and Eurasia. The tiny brownish leaves hardly reach 1cm (0.4in) in length, and the flower is scarcely 9mm (0.35in), pale violet to white, yellow-veined with two yellow spots on the lower lip. I have not heard of

P. gypsicola in flower

anyone who grows this, but as it comes from acid bogland try it in a mixture of 2 parts moss peat to 1 part sand. Two other species which may not yet be in cultivation are *P. variegata* from Siberia, with small rosettes of nearly round leaves and pale blue and yellow flowers pencilled in violet; and the Japanese *P. ramose*, which is curious in that its flowering stalk has two to three branches, each bearing a single white flower. Its spoon-shaped leaves are in a rosette to about 2.3cm (0.9in) in diameter.

Distinctly different from all the above is *P. vallisneriifolia* from the Sierra de Cazorla and other areas in southern Spain. Its long and extremely narrow outer leaves can reach as much as 20cm (nearly 8in) in length, making it the giant of

European species. The flowers are about the same sizes as those of *P. grandiflora*, but of soft lilac-blue, the bases of the lips and throat being white and hairy. This is a plant for the cool greenhouse, and it must be shaded from direct sun. Because of the enormous size of its rosette, use a deep plastic planting box or similar container. Use the same compost as recommended for *P. longifolia*, and embed small pieces of limestone tufa in the surface of the compost. Disturb the mother plant as little as possible. It is unusual in propagating itself from stolons, and the young plants may be later potted up. I have not tried it from seed.

The winter rosette of *P. gypsicola* among the remains of the summer leaves and the bodies of greenhouse whitefly

OTHER EUROPEAN SPECIES

A minority of European butterworts do not produce winter resting buds, and retain the same kind of rosette throughout the year.

The Pale Butterwort *P. lusitanica* occurs in milder parts of Western Europe, including the western parts of the British Isles, and in North Africa. It is a pretty species which likes to grow on naked black peat over or around which water is seeping. The leaves are narrowly elliptical, usually much less than 2cm (0.78in) long, and their margins are so far incurved that often little of the upper leaf surface is visible. They are almost transparent, of bluish-green, and the hair-like network of red veins is conspicuous, but in sunny places they assume a pinkish hue. The plentifully produced pale lilac-pink flowers are up to 5mm (0.2in) long, and the corolla almost trumpet-shaped in profile, with a downward directed spur. This is a short-lived perennial which hates root disturbance. It is, therefore, best raised from seed sown on the surface of a mixture of 3 parts moss peat to 1 part horticultural sand. I use a 12.5cm (5in) dwarf pot. The plant grows well in the coolhouse if protected from direct strong sunlight. Water on the tray system. It produces seed without needing hand pollination.

Pinguicula hirtiflora is a rarity from southern Italy and the eastern Mediterranean. Its flat rosettes of elliptical leaves somewhat resemble those of *P. vulgaris*, but such a connection is belied by the flowers. In the form I grow, these are large and beautiful, with lilac-violet lobes becoming snow white in their lower parts, while the throat is brilliant orange. At best a short-lived perennial, this is a plant which you will need to hand-pollinate and resow (see page 85). Grow it in a mixture of 3 parts moss peat to 1 part horticultural sand in the coolhouse. It does not object to direct sun, providing summer shading has been applied to the glass. Water on the tray system. Closely related to this is *P. crystalline* from the Troodos Mountains in Cyprus. The rosettes are up to 5cm (2in) wide, the leaves elliptically oblong, and the large flowers range from soft rose to pale blue. Young plants will respond to the same treatment as for *P. hirtiflora*.

SPECIES FROM CENTRAL AMERICA AND THE CARIBBEAN

Even within a race of almost unfailingly lovely species, the butterworts of Central America and the Caribbean are, with few exceptions, remarkable for their outstanding beauty. Why this should be so is something of a mystery, particularly as by no means all of them are closely related. Some have the peculiarity of producing distinctly different leaves at different times of the year.

The 'summer rosette' consists of typical butterwort foliage which is sticky-glanded and carnivorous, while in the drought-resistant 'winter rosette' the leaves are small to tiny, thick and succulent, the rosette often resembling a houseleek (*Sempervivum*). There are no sticky glands and the leaf is not carnivorous. Other species do not produce a winter rosette and have the typical butterwort foliage throughout the year. The leaf rosettes can be extremely fine, yet the crowning glory of most species is in their flowers, which many produce abundantly. Often large, these are not only remarkable for the range and subtlety of their colours, but (especially in the so-called 'orchid-flowered species') for their purity and brightness.

Some species are found in mossy forests on the mountains, where they are dampened for most of the year by persistent mists. Here they are not only found on the forest floor but growing epiphytically upon the mossy tree trunks, *P. moranensis* being such a plant. At least two species from the Caribbean are true epiphytes. Others experience wet conditions for much of the year, but are also subjected to a period of extreme drought, surviving this by means of an extra-succulent winter rosette, an example being *P. gypsicola*.

General cultivation None of the species is difficult. While the numerous *P. moranensis* forms, *P. agnata*, *P. gypsicola* and their hybrids will grow satisfactorily in the coolhouse, they grow much better in warm greenhouse temperatures, in similar temperatures in the heated terrarium, or indoors in a sunny window, and this is best for all other species. Use a 12.5cm (5in) pot, regardless of the size of species. This may accommodate one large plant or a group of one of the smaller species. For compost use a mixture of 4 parts moss peat, 1 part horticultural sand, and 2 parts John Innes Compost No. 2. Alternatively you may use 3 parts moss peat to 1 part sand, only in this case it is advisable to spray the foliage every two weeks in the summer with a suitable foliar feed, such as weak Orchidquick as recommended for *Nepenthes* (see page 123).

Potting should be done in spring or early summer, just as the first summer leaves are seen to be coming into growth. Never pot when the plants are in their full summer growth if you can help it, for the root system is delicate and if damaged will not recuperate at that time, often leading to the loss of a specimen. Though the soil in the pot should be well firmed, you should place it gently around the roots of the plants on account of this fragility. Shading should always be applied to the glass in late spring or earliest summer, for the foliage is yellowed by strong sunlight, and can be easily burnt. Water on the tray system, using soft water. In winter leave the tray dry, putting only enough water in it for the pots to absorb, so that the compost in winter is moist rather than wet, but permanent water is restored to the tray as soon as the summer leaves come into growth.

Exceptions are *P. gypsicola*, its hybrid *P. moranensis x P. gypsicola*, and no doubt other hybrids to which it is a parent, for in these the compost must be allowed to become bone-dry in the winter rosette stage, and must so remain until the spring, or until the summer foliage is seen to be emerging from the centre, when the pot must be returned to the water tray.

PROPAGATION

The two simplest methods are division and seed.

Division should be done only in spring, and then only if your plant clearly consists of a clump of not less than four crowns, for where there are less, injury is often caused.

Seed is best sown fresh on the surface of a compost of 3 parts moss peat, 1 part

The delicate beauty of Harald Weiner's
P. 'species nova No. 4'

horticultural sand, using a dwarf pot or plastic seed box. Otherwise treat as for the mature plant. Note that with few exceptions the flower must be hand-pollinated; the method for carrying this out is given on page 85. Instead of pollinating one flower with another of the same species, you may care to attempt a cross with the pollen of another species. In this case be meticulous about keeping a record and labelling the pollinated seed-head appropriately. In this way you may raise a new hybrid, or at least a seedling which show qualities lacking in others of the same parentage.

Leaf cuttings The advantage of this over division is that more plants can be raised at one time; and over seed, that young plants often reach maturity within less than one year. They are most successful in the case of those species that produced winter rosettes, when only the winter leaves should be used; these remain accessible and healthy for some time after the summer leaves are formed. But whatever the type, the cuttings should be taken in late spring or early summer, so that you may repot the parent plant.

Lift the plant from its compost and gently pull away, in a slightly downwards direction, healthy leaves from the outer part of the rosette. If they are taken from

P. esseriana

elsewhere you will not be able to pull them away without causing damage to the plant and/or the leaf base, and they must in any case never be taken from near the centre of the plant. The leaves are brittle, so make the break a clean one. Put the leaves the correct way up on a clean surface for twenty minutes, to allow the break to seal.

Meanwhile prepare a compost of 3 parts moss peat to 1 part horticultural peat. Use no John Innes. Put this compost in 12.5cm (5in) dwarf pots, firm, and see that the surface is very level. Lay the leaves, upper surface uppermost, on the surface, spacing them so that they do not touch one another. With a pencil or similar object shift a minute amount of compost to just cover the break wound in each cutting. Place the pot in a saucer of soft water until the surface of the compost is seen to be moist, then remove, and either place the pot in the cool or, preferably, warm greenhouse in a position shaded from direct sun, or in a light place in the house, and cover with a propagating cover. Alternatively, place in a heated terrarium at 18.5–24°C (65–75°F), and if high humidity is maintained the propagator cover is not necessary.

Regularly inspect, removing any leaves which show signs of rotting. Some leaves can be expected to bud within weeks, others may take months. These buds arise usually, but not always, from around the base of the cutting. Unless in a very humid atmosphere, leave the cover over the pot until nice, well-rooted plantlets have been formed. Then individually remove these as they become ready, and plant in full-size pots, being treated in every way as the adult plant, but keep the potted plant under a propagating cover for its first ten days to encourage it to settle. Sometimes a leaf may form several little plants, which may be difficult to divide without hurting one or more of the plantlets. In this case, it is best to pot up, dividing the clump the following spring.

Pests and diseases Cultivated plants appear to keep relatively free of diseases. Grey Mould (*Botrytis cinerea*) can affect them, but this is almost always secondary to pest attack. Treat as for *Sarracenia* (see page 50). Slugs, woodlice, and more occasionally snails, are normally the worst. Treat again as for *Sarracenia*. A very annoying pest, the Tarsonemid Mite, has made its unwelcome appearance in some collections. These creatures are so minute that they can only be observed with a strong lens or microscope, but you will usually be made aware of their presence by the symptoms. They live only in the very centre of the rosette amongst the small developing foliage. They are harmless enough in summer when plant growth is fast enough to outstrip any real damage, and they do not usually hurt species which retain one rosette form. It is among those which produce winter rosettes that the trouble lies, for in these rosettes growth is so slow that the creatures have time to cause much destruction to the embryo leaf. These become distorted, often failing to develop properly, and are often of a paler or unhealthy colour. All too often the centre of the plant will eventually die, and with it the whole plant. Though difficult to entirely eradicate, it is now easily controlled with 'Dicofol' (or Better Dicofol and Tetradifon).

Occasionally the roots may be attacked by nematodes, which again can cause the death of the plant, especially if it is already under attach from tarsonemids. Rotting of roots and plant centres without any sign of a visible soil pest would indicate its probable presence. While a proven soil insecticide such as Gamma HCH will discourage their attacks, a very effective control is Temik – a poison. In view of its extreme toxicity this is supplied only in large quantities, and only to professional nurserymen. If you do consider using it, remember it can enter the body directly through the skin by simple contact. Never use it where children might touch the soil. The instructions supplied with the compound should be followed exactly.

THE SPECIES

Among the most beautiful of the species are those belonging to what the botanists call the Orchiosanthus section – the Orchid-flowered butterworts, to the gardener (*PP. moranensis, macrophylla, gypsicola, cyclosecta, oblongiloba* and *colinemsis*). All produce summer and winter rosettes.

P. moranensis has long been cultivated as *P. caudate*, or *P. bakeriana*, but the latter must now be regarded as either an unidentified geographical form or horticultural variety of the species. This variety has large, light-green, oval summer leaves, the rosettes being up to 20cm (8in) wide. Each produces several large flowers not only in summer but again for a period in winter. They are flat-faced, up to 5cm (2in) long and nearly as wide, the upper lip is formed by two broad petal-like lobes, the lower one by three. These are deep cyclamen-pink, paling somewhat with age. The base of each lobe is touched and veined with crimson, while the narrow throat is flecked with white. One bloom may remain in prime condition for up to six weeks. Some distinct horticultural forms of this variety exist, including the robust and fine-flowered cultivar, var. *caudate* 'Superba'.

Geographical forms of this species show an astonishing range of variation, especially in flower, their colours passing from white through pale pink to deepest orchid-purple and violet-blue, their lobes being anything from narrowly strap-shaped to wide and petal-like in form. They are usually named after the geographical area in which they have been found.

In 'Vera Cruz' the flower is of similar form to var. *caudate*, but it is of deep rose with more substantial basal marking. A form of doubtful origin and name, 'Mexicana' has short, round-ended lobes of orchid-purple, with a solitary white touch below the throat. Of very distinct appearance, *P. moranensis* var. *rosei* was until recently regarded as a separate species. Its large, abundantly produced flowers are in a vivid shade of royal purple, while its elliptical, somewhat pointed, leaves are a reddish to coppery green. There are many other fine forms from the wild; one with fine white flowers has entered cultivation and should be available from nurseries.

P. colimensis could easily be confused with the last species in leaf, which is, however, rather smaller and rounder. The flowers are even larger, of a beautiful deep rose, and the light pink spur is unusually long. *P. oblongiloba* has small, neat summer rosettes seldom exceeding 5cm (2in) across, pale green, copper-tinted, spatula-shaped leaves, but with comparatively large flowers of about the same width. These are violet-purple with oblong lobes, narrowing markedly almost to a point, and a long, downward-pointing spur. Even smaller in its summer rosette is little *P. cyclosecta*. These may not exceed 2cm (0.78in), and consists of many spatula-shaped to oval leaves. The flowers may exceed in diameter that of the rosette itself, and have lobes of pure mallow-purple, with a white throat in which the rust-red stigmas provide a conspicuous eye.

CURIOUS FOLIAGE

The two remaining members of this section are remarkable for their curious foliage. In *P. gypsicola* the summer leaves are long and lance-shaped, up to 6.5cm (2.55in) long by 2.5mm (0.1in) at their widest. Semi-erect and somewhat in-curved, they unroll from their ends fern-fashion and have flowers similar to those of *P. moranensis* with somewhat narrow lobes of soft purply pink with darker veins.

The summer leaves of *P. macrophylla* are borne aloft, up to 14cm (5.5in) long, and consist of an oval to roundish blade held on a distinct stalk which is nearly as long as, or longer than, the blade. The flowers are rich violet-purple, up to 5cm (2in) across, and have long, downward-pointing spurs.

Of others, one of my favourites is that which Mr Harald Weiner catalogues as 'species nova No. 4'. This species has neat little summer rosettes up to 7cm (2.75in) in diameter. The leaves are curiously shaped, the base being narrow and strap-like, gradually widening until they open out in the top third into an almost perfect circle. The several flowers are up to 1.3cm (0.5in) wide, and are of a lovely shade of pale milky violet with a wide throat of dark violet. *P. ehlersae* has unusually attractive leaves in rosettes 3.5cm (1.4in) wide. They are pale coppery pink, in contrast to the pale-green undersides of the rolled edges. The flowers are surprisingly large, up to 2.5cm (1in) wide, of rose-purple with a white throat. *P. esseriana*, another small grower with beautiful rosettes to 2.5cm (1in) in diameter. They consist of up to sixty pale green spatula-shaped leaves, arranged formally as in an *Echeveria*. Its flowers are up to 2cm (0.78in) wide, with broadly wedge-shaped lobes of rose-purple, graduating to light lobelia-violet towards the extremities. In *P. parvifolia* the summer rosettes of oblong-oval leaves can reach a diameter of 2.5cm (1in). The purplish-blue, white-throated flowers can be even wider. There is also a white-flowered form.

P. sharpii is unusual in being an annual, and is a miniature with flat rosettes of broadly oval leaves to 3.3cm (1.3in) in diameter. Its dainty white flowers are only 1cm (0.4in) long, and much resemble those of *P. lusitanica* in profile. It is self-pollinating and is easily propagated from seed. Two other species are, firstly, *P. heterophylla*, which is an interesting plant with a summer rosette consisting of three distinct leaf shapes. The outer ones are oval to oblong, to 2.5cm (1in) long, while the inner ones are narrowly lance-shaped, to 9cm (3.5in). The large flowers may be pale rose to violet, purple or white according to form. The second candidate is *P. imitatrix*, which has summer rosettes to 9cm (3.5in) across, with narrowly oblong to lance-shaped leaves. The flowers are purple.

Of those that do not form winter rosettes, *P. lilacina* has foliage somewhat like *P. moranensis*, except that the edges point down rather than up. The flowers are quite large, of lilac blue, and show their close relationship with the majority of species of the south-east United States by their well-developed yellow palates. The lobes have roundish ends and the mouth of the throat is bluish.

P. agnata has rather narrow, almost strap-shaped leaves with rounded ends. They are unusually thick and succulent, and form rosettes to 13cm (5in) in diameter. The medium-sized, wide-throated flowers are mauve-blue, gradually deepening to pale violet around the margins of the lobes, and there are two deep flecks at the base of each. The throat is greenish. A quite splendid species of recent introduction is *P. zecheri*. Its domed rosettes are up to 10cm (4in) in diameter, and consist of somewhat arched, narrowly elliptical, bright-green leaves. The large, abundantly produced flowers are magnificent. They are of a deep, intense violet-purple contrasted with a white throat, from which lighter and darker veins radiate. I have not grown *P. crenatiloba*; the oval leaves form a rosette to 2.5cm (1in) in diameter. The tiny flowers are to 4.5mm (0.17in) long in perfect scale, and are off-white to palest purplish white; there is a yellow palate and the wide throat is blotched with yellow.

A short distance across the Caribbean, in Cuba and Haiti, other beautiful species are found. There is *P. filifolia* and others in cultivation that are subjects for the warm greenhouse or heated terrarium. Of west Cuban species, *P. jackii* has pale yellowish-green, broadly oval leaves forming rosettes to 10cm (4in) wide. The large flowers are deep blue with wide whitish, sometimes purple-tinted throats. *P. benedicta* has rosettes to 3cm (1.2in) of narrowly obovate leaves, and medium-sized flowers of a smokey lilac blue. *P. albida* has roundishly elliptical, pale yellowish-green leaves in rosettes to about 6cm (2.3in) wide. The pretty flowers have snow-white lobes of equal length, giving the impression of a *Primula* when seen from the front, and there is even an orange 'eye' in the form of a star, formed by the throat. Of very different appearance, *P. filifolia* has numerous erect thread-like (filiform) leaves to 15cm (6in). Above these the flowers may be white, blue to purple, or rose to lilac, for there are many colour forms.

We now come to two unusual and interesting species, for both are epiphytic, growing only upon trees. *P. lignicola* is again from western Cuba, where it is found attached to twigs and branchlets. The little rosettes of narrowly elliptical, pale-green leaves are up to 2cm (0.78in) across, from which grow several scapes of large beautiful white flowers very similar to those of *P. albida*. *P. cladophila* is found in the central mountains of Haiti in mossy forest, where it is often found on the tops of branches. The narrow lance-shaped leaves are in rosettes to 6cm (2.3in) across, and the flowers are again white. I imagine that both species might respond to being grown in a mixture of orchid bark, Perlite and moss peat in equal proportions.

There is much scope for the judicious and selective hybridising amongst the Central American and Caribbean species, and it is my belief that these plants will achieve a horticultural importance in time approaching or even equalling that of the African Violet (*Saintpaulia*). At the time of writing we are only at the beginning, yet a number of fine named hybrids have appeared. Of these I would mention *P. x* 'Sethos' (*P. moranensis x P. ehlersae*), a fine, very floriferous clone with large orchid-purple flowers with a many-rayed mouth like a white star; *P. x* 'Weser', of the same parentage and with rather similar flowers, has a solitary white streak down the central lower lobe and dark veins. *P. x* 'Tina' has large wide-throated flowers of mauve, the bases of the lobes being heavily streaked in violet with a pale-green throat, and is a hybrid of *P. agnata x P. zecheri*. Mr G.A. Sargent has crossed *P. moranensis* var. *caudate* with *P. gypsicola*. The clone he gave me produced numerous rich lilac flowers over curiously bendy, strap-shaped leaves. The winter rosettes are enormous, and at that time they must be kept bone dry. *P. x* 'Hamelyn' and *P. x* 'Mitla' are of the *P. gypsicola x P.* 'Hamburg' cross, and both differ in their wider *moranensis*-like foliage and in not producing the large winter rosettes of *P. x* 'George Sargent'. *P. moranensis* var. *rosei* was crossed with *P. moranensis* var. *caudata* at Kew many years ago. This produced the fine *P. x kewensis*, with pale coppery foliage and long-spurred flowers of a deeper colour than in var. *caudate*.

BUTTERWORTS OF THE SOUTH-EAST UNITED STATES

These are principally plants of the wet coastal plains. All produce beautiful flowers in a wide range of colours, characterized by a hairy beard situated on the lower front opening of the throat and projecting conspicuously outwards in some species.

Cultivation These are at home in the coolhouse. They require high humidity and are best grown under a propagating cover for this reason. Alternatively, you may grow them in an unheated terrarium on a window-sill or under fluorescent lights, but in all cases they must be protected from direct sunlight.

Use a compost of 2 parts moss peat to 1 part horticultural sand. They are by nature short-lived, and adult plants often die when transplanted, so it is advisable to plant into permanent quarters when still young. All are easily raised from seed scattered on the surface of the same compost, using plastic seed boxes covered with a propagating cover, watering on the tray system and protecting from direct sunlight. Sow sparsely and transplant to their permanent pots when the rosettes are about 1cm (0.4in) in diameter. To produce seed, the flowers must be hand-pollinated (see page 85). *P. primuliflora* has the obliging habit of forming buds at the tips of its older leaves where these touch the ground. These soon form little plants which may be potted up. *P. ionantha* will also do this occasionally and *P. planifolia* even less frequently.

THE SPECIES

The Yellow Butterwort *P. lutea* is unusual in the bright chrome-yellow coloration of its fine flowers, which are to 3.5cm (1.4in) long, with a projecting beard. The pale green oval-pointed leaves are in rosettes to 12cm (4.7in) diameter. The Violet Butterwort *P. caerulea* has almost identical foliage, but the flowers are typically pale violet, richly pencilled with parallel veins of deep violet, with a greenish-cream beard. This is a lovely form, preferable to the less common dark-purple or white forms. The leaves of *P. primuliflora* are very similar, and the flowers are of a beautiful shade of rose pink. The white bases of the lobes form a central ring within which the tube and projecting beard form a bright yellow eye, the frontal effect being very like a pink primrose, hence the specific name. In *P. ionantha* the leaf rosette is again similar. Though the flowers are typically white with a pink centre, forms occur also with faint-violet flowers with deep-violet centres. There is a projecting yellow beard. All the above need 12.5cm (5in) dwarf pots.

The giant of the group is *P. planifolia*, in which the elliptical-pointed leaves may form rosettes to 15cm (6in) in diameter. Usually of an attractive dull reddish to purple tint, they are occasionally green. The flowers are light pink with dark pink centres and projecting yellow beards. Each lobe is deeply cut down its centre, giving the impression of a many-petalled flower. Use a wide container – a 15cm (6in) dwarf pot will suffice.

In complete contrast is tiny *P. pumila*, whose pale-green rosettes will scarcely reach a diameter of 2cm (0.78in), with flowers in perfect scale. These are usually white with yellow beards, but forms with both yellow and pink flowers are found in Florida. A 12.5cm (5in) dwarf pot will accommodate seven plants nicely.

SOME SOUTH AMERICAN BUTTERWORTS

Most are best placed in the coolhouse, watered on the tray system in a moss peat and sand compost. *P. chilensis* grows in wet mossy places in the Andes in Chile and Argentina, and has oval leaves in rosettes to 4.4cm (1.7in) across. The small flowers vary from white with violet veins to deep blue. *P. calyptrate* favours mossy, marshy places in the Andes in Ecuador and Colombia. Its oblong-oval leaves are in rosettes to 5.5cm (2.2in) diameter, and it has small violet-purple flowers. *P. involuta* inhabits cold, wet places in the Andes of Peru and Bolivia. Its rosettes are up to 4.8cm (1.9in) wide, the leaves oval-oblong, and the small flowers are pale to deep violet or white. The rare *P. elongata* is a native of Venezuela and Colombia, where it is said to inhabit marshy, cool and sandy places. Unlike the others this plant has distinct summer and winter rosettes, like many of the Central American species, and might perhaps respond to similar treatment. While the leaves of the winter rosette are numerous, short and succulent, those of the summer growth are very different. These are lance-shaped to as much as 15cm (6in) long by as little as 0.5–1cm (0.2–0.4in) wide, and semi to fully erect. The flowers are of medium size on scapes taller than the foliage. They are of violet to pale violet, veined in blue with a wide throat; this is a fascinating species.

Coming from the inhospitable and immensely variable climate of the extreme southern part of the continent, *P. Antarctica* favours marshy places in coastal areas and on the western islands. The oval-oblong leaves are borne in a rosette to 3.5cm (1.4in) wide, and the plant has small purple flowers.

The Forked Trap: Genlisea

*G*enlisea is a strange semi-aquatic plant which resembles no other carnivorous genus in trap structure, although it is closely related to the bladderworts *Utricularia*. Of the fourteen known species, five have been recorded in various parts of tropical and sub-tropical Africa, while the other nine are native to South and Central America and Cuba. Amongst the species and their forms the trap can vary in length from 2.5–15cm (1–6in), and somewhat resembles a two-pronged fork. These prongs are normally suspended in waterlogged moss or mud. Where the two prongs meet there is a narrow slit-like entrance, and this is continued in a spiral down both prongs. The mechanism of the trap was fairly compared by Charles Darwin to that of the eel trap. Small creatures can enter the slit at any point, when they will find themselves in a one-way tunnel. They are guided into the main tube of the trap, lined with rings of hairs which prevent passage back to the outside, and from thence into the bulb-shaped object. This can be likened to a stomach, for in it are glands which secrete juices over the victim, digesting the soft parts of its body, the resulting nutrients then being absorbed into the plant. The foliage blades are spoon-shaped to linear in form, while the long, slender flower stalks bear one to several attractive two-lipped, toadflax-like flowers, which much resemble those of some of their bladderwort relatives.

Cultivation With slight modification use the method adopted by Phillip Jacobs; keep it in warm humid conditions in a shallow plastic tray 15 x 10 x 5cm (6 x 4 x 2in) deep. Cover the bottom with a shallow layer of river sand for drainage in winter and then fill the box with live sphagnum moss mixed with a little moss peat. In summer (always using soft water) keep the water level with the surface of the sphagnum and of the leaf rosette, and keep a day temperature of between 20 and

FRASER LAMOND OF BERARIO, SOUTH AFRICA

'My plant is *G. hispidula* ssp. *hispidula* and was given me by Phillip Jacobs of Johannesburg from material collected in the Transvaal. There it occurs mainly in the southern and eastern parts, here it grows in areas of high rainfall in marshes and wet places, often in sopping conditions, and in company with such plants as *Drosera burkeana* and *D. diellsiana*. My plant forms small rosettes of leaves about 5–6cm (2–2.3in) across, each leaf being 1.5–2cm (0.6–0.78in) long, while the traps themselves are about 1.5cm (0.6in) long. My plant has yet to flower, but from information gleaned in the herbarium at the Botanical Research Institute in Pretoria I have found that the scape is up to 25cm (nearly 10in) long and that the flowers are mauvy pink, but that both yellow- and white-flowered forms occasionally occur also.'

30°C (68–86°F), though it sometimes rises above this, and a night minimum of 10°C (50°F). In winter, keep the sphagnum damp only, with a hot day temperature of 30°C (86°F), but a much cooler night temperature of 5°C (41°F) minimum. Early morning sun with 50 per cent shading around the middle of the day, i.e. semi-shade.

Some, probably all, of the species will be happy in a heated terrarium or stovehouse.

The Bladderworts: Utricularia

There are over 250 species of bladderwort, from many parts of the world, including aquatic, terrestrial and tree-dwelling (epiphytic) species in their ranks. They are extraordinary in possessing no roots (the root-like processes which some possess being stems), and also in having no true leaves. Foliage, which is often very leaf-like, consists in fact of wonderfully modified shoots. The traps probably represent much-modified leaves, as the bracts on the flowering stalks undoubtedly do.

The bladderworts are perhaps the most interesting of all carnivorous plants, on account of the structure and mechanism of the trap which far outstrips that of the Venus Fly Trap in the sheer wonder of its design and efficiency.

TRAPDOOR

The little bladder-like traps are of somewhat oval shape and usually more or less transparent. There is only one entrance at one end and this is normally sealed by a Trapdoor with several trigger hairs on its outside. A small swimming creature touching one of these will trip the mechanism. The pressure on the hair buckles the door, thus releasing a partial vacuum within the trap, so that the door opens inwards, letting in a rush of water which carries the victim in with it. Now, with the release of the vacuum, the door immediately swings back to its original shut position and the victim is a prisoner. The entire action has taken place in something in the region of a ten-thousandth to fifteen-thousandth of a second. The partial vacuum is restored within about twenty minutes, and the trap is then ready to catch another animal. The prey soon dies, and is digested by secreted juices.

People often wonder how those species which are not aquatic catch prey. Such plants grow in very wet soil, moss or detritus, so the traps are able to catch organisms which swim about in water either held by capillary attraction or by a high water-table. But apart from the interest of their traps, which become even more fascinating if you are able to examine them under the microscope, you may well find many species worth growing for the variety and beauty of their two-lipped and spurred flowers, which may resemble tiny toadflaxes (*Linaria*) at one extreme, or large and beautiful orchids at the other.

TERRESTRIAL BLADDERWORTS

All the ground-dwelling species favour acid to occasionally neutral soils, usually of a peaty and/or sandy nature. Unless otherwise stated I have grown mine in a

Terrestrial bladderwort *U. sandersonii*

Terrestrial bladderwort *U. subuluta*

compost of 2 parts moss peat to 1 part horticultural sand, and favour 10cm (4in) pots, or 12.5cm (5in) dwarf pots, watering on the tray system. If grown in direct sunlight the glass should have a good coating of shading in summer; alternatively, the plants may with few exceptions be grown in complete shade but a good light, and on south- or west-facing window-sills. A winter minimum of 4°C (40°F) is satisfactory for most. All are best propagated from divisions taken in the height of the growing season, and never in autumn or winter. It is wise to start new colonies at least biennially, as vigour tends to diminish after that time.

The flowers in this group tend to resemble toadflaxes, occur in many colours, and while a large number of others have yet to be introduced to cultivation the following are all attractive and worth growing.

THE SPECIES

U. sandersonii is a little beauty from South Africa, smothering itself with myriads of soft wisteria-blue flowers above lettuce-green foliage. Each short scape bears up to seven of these. The upper lip is divided into two long and narrow lobes with violet central veins, and the lower lip is petticoat shaped, while the long spur curves downwards and then forwards beneath this. Also from the same country, *U. livida* has longer scapes, to 2cm (0.78in), bearing up to eight substantial flowers. Though the upper lip is minute, the lower lip is large and broadly tongue-shaped. It is of pale violet with a creamy white palate touched with a central yellowish-green streak. Like the last, it is exceedingly floriferous. Best kept in full sun, muted by shading on the glass in summer, for when in shade the flowers open white. *U. pubescens* (syn. *U. peltata*) occurs in India, Africa and South America, and has round foliage like numerous tiny green buttons scattered over the soil. The scape is surprisingly tall, to 25cm (10in), and bears several large and beautiful lilac flowers with a darker palate touched with yellow and white, each about 12cm (4.72in) in diameter. From the US, *U. subulata* has several delicate, rich-yellow blooms on blackish-purple stems about 7.5cm (3in) high. These are so hair-like that from a distance the blooms seem to be floating in the air. *U. monanthos* is different from all other species here listed in being alpine, coming from the mountains of Australia, Tasmania and New Zealand. In England it seems to be quite hardy, but thrives best in the coolhouse. Said to be a shy flowerer, a form (from the Southern Alps of New Zealand) has never disappointed me. The flowers are borne singly per scape just above the ground, and have an extra large lower lip which is tear-shaped and of a lovely shade of slate-blue, with a conspicuous fleck of chrome yellow on its palate.

The above species all make good 'starters'. Once you have them in your collection you might find these plants have a curious hold over you. Try *U. graminifolia* from India and the Far East, which is covered in late summer with short scapes of several powder blue flowers. It prefers a minimum temperature of 10°C (50°F). *U. laterifolia* from Australia has scapes of several soft violet-blue flowers touched on the white palate with yellow. *U. capensis* is a delightful miniature from South Africa, which regrettably may be known in future under its hideous synonym of *U. bisquamata*. Its scapes, to about 2.5cm (1in), bear proportionately small flowers, which in the commonly cultivated form are in a combination of violet, orange, white and yellow. There is a still more minute and attractive form with numerous pure white flowers.

RED COATS AND FAMILY APRONS

Altogether different is the Western Australian *U. menziesii*, known locally as 'Red Coats' on account of the bright-red colour of its large, bizarre yet beautiful flowers, which are borne singly. It is a shy flowerer, and be warned that while slugs have no appetite for the leaves they have a passion for the flowering scapes, and will find them if they have to travel even some distance. They are unusual in being tuber-forming and in having a dormant period. Treat as other terrestrial bladderworts, but allow the pot to gradually dry out when the foliage is seen to be dying back. Keep it in the same position but dry until the first new leaves start to emerge, when the pot should again stand in water.

Propagate by division only when you have a large clump, which may take years to build up, and do this in the earliest stages of growth only. *U. praelonga* of Brazil bears two leaf types simultaneously, one narrow and grass-like to 23cm (9in), the other small, round, and pressed to the ground. The sprays of fairly large, rich yellow flowers reach 46cm (18in). Grow this in pure live sphagnum in a 12.5cm (5in) pot.

Known as 'Fairy Aprons' in its native Australia, *U. dichotoma* is a beautiful plant. The substantial flowers are borne in opposite pairs, several to a scape to 30cm (12in) tall. Forms occur in the wild from mauve to purple, those in cultivation being generally violet with white and yellow palates. Subtropical, it should have a winter minimum of 15.5°C (60°F), and likes a high water-level, being often amphibious in nature. *U. novae-zealandiae* from New Zealand is botanically distinct, but is so similar as to be easily confused. It should be given identical treatment.

AMPHIBIOUS BLADDERWORTS

Many species favour low-lying areas which may be subject to prolonged periods of shallow flooding, and in this sense might be described as being terrestrials disposed to an amphibious state, but the following species are truly so. The pots should be placed in a container deep enough to allow them to be submerged at times. Unless stated otherwise, keep the water-level slightly lower than, or level with, that of the compost surface most of the time, occasionally (but only after they are well established) raising this to up to 2.5cm (1in) above this level for two or three weeks. A few weeks later, introduce live water fleas to the water (from many aquarium shops), which both help to keep the water clear and provide food during the submerged periods. Increase by division in spring or early summer. All require coolhouse conditions. Use 12.5cm (5in) dwarf pots.

THE SPECIES

U. prehensilis has tall scapes to about 30cm (12in) high, which are unusual in their method of climbing and twining. They bear up to several medium-sized, bright-yellow flowers. The foliage is narrowly strap-shaped, of bright lettuce-green. This is a species that, once well established, should be kept permanently submerged, at first under very shallow water, gradually raising this to a depth of 2.5cm (1in) or so. Split bamboos will provide support for the climbing flowering stems. It occurs in many parts of Africa.

U. spiralis, also from Africa, has similar foliage but should be given standard treatment. The scape can be twining, or it may be straight and rather shorter. The form in general cultivation is of the latter type, and has up to five pale-purple

The Horned Bladderwort *U. cornuta*

flowers. *U. caerulea* ranges from India to Japan and Australia, and again has rather similar foliage. The scapes are up to about 18cm (7in) high, and bear several purplish-blue flowers. The Horned Bladderwort *U. cornuta* from the US has strong flower stalks to 30cm (12in), bearing several quite large and showy, rich yellow flowers with downward pointing spurs and grassy, very narrow foliage. Though botanically distinct, *U. juncea* is horticulturally almost identical but rather smaller, and is again from the US, as is little *U. resupinata*, the Reversed Bladderwort, which has tiny narrow foliage and scapes to about 10cm (4in). These bear several flowers of a delicate lilac pink. In nature it favours very shallow water never more than 5cm (2in) deep. Always rare and localized in nature, I was fortunate once to find it in full flower by the shore of Lake Killimmee in central Florida. Here, motivated by ripples, they appeared to dance in their tens of thousands above the shallow water like strange flying insects.

From India and Sri Lanka *U. reticulata* needs a warm greenhouse or heated terrarium, but otherwise similar treatment. It has twining scapes to 30cm (12in) which bear up to seven large purple flowers with attractively veined white palates. These stems will need the support of a split bamboo. *U. tricolor* from Brazil, Venezuela, Colombia and Paraguay is the odd one out, with its distinctive short-stemmed, kidney-shaped to roundish foliage. The blades are up to 3cm (1.2 in) across, but usually much less, and often more or less prostrate. The young scapes at first resemble the leaves of rushes, growing up to 46cm (18in) and bear several beautiful flowers, about 2cm (0.78in) across, of pale violet with deep violet around the large white palate, which is touched with yellow.

EPIPHYTIC AND SIMILAR BLADDERWORTS

An epiphyte is a plant that grows on another. Of the epiphytic bladderworts, most grow on trees in rainforests, where their stolons get a foothold in moss, bark and detritus, but two live on bromeliads. They are not parasites, and do no harm to their hosts. Among these species are found those with the largest and most magnificent of flowers, which can compare reasonably with the finest orchids. Indeed, they are often mistaken for these, which they somewhat resemble and, like them, the flowers can last in beauty for several weeks. These are splendid plants, well worth growing and not at all difficult.

Cultivation All those listed will succeed in the coolhouse, though they do better in the warmhouse or in the unheated terrarium indoors. They certainly do appreciate a very high humidity, but this is by no means essential. The foliage is easily affected by strong sunlight, and shading must always be applied to the glass in summer. The preferable compost consists of 2 parts orchid bark, 2 parts moss peat, 1 part Perlite and a little horticultural sand. Water on the tray system.

Propagation is by division during full growth in early summer. Note that divisions taken at other times often die and can kill the parent plant. This is best done only when you have a large clump, and you should try to take the largest portions you can, including as much foliage as you can on each piece. It is worth pointing out that colonies should not be disturbed for division or any other purpose if you wish them to flower. Large, well-established and undisturbed clumps tend to bloom best. Grow and treat as for the parent plant.

Pests and diseases Aphids are the only kind which have caused trouble, and they are safely controlled with any good greenhouse aphicide. Remove all dead foliage, especially when plants are in the enclosed humid conditions of the terrarium.

THE SPECIES

From Brazil, *U. longifolia* has light green, irregularly strap-shaped foliage up to 15cm (6in) long, narrowing almost to a stalk at the base, which may die away for a

U. alpina. This epiphyte will carry up to four white flowers

The orchid-like *U. nephrophylla*

period in winter. The scapes are up to 60cm (24in) tall and bear in the typical form up to ten large lilac-mauve to lilac-pink flowers with a golden blotch on the palate. Variable in nature, a form with violet-blue flowers, var. *forgetiana*, was once in cultivation and this deserves to be rediscovered. Best grown in a 25cm (10in) dwarf pot or orchid basket, and left undisturbed if you wish it to flower. *U. alpina* (syn. *U. montana*) grows in the West Indies, Central and South America. Its foliage is light green, to about 15cm (6in), paddle-shaped and sharply pointed. The scape is up to 30cm (12in) and bears up to four somewhat nodding flowers perhaps 3.5cm (1.4in) in diameter, white to cream in colour with an orange-yellow palate. Well-established plants form many egg-shaped ground tubers up to 2.5cm (1in) long. Give this a 12.5cm (5in) pot or larger, and allow it to colonize.

Excellent in the unheated terrarium.

U. endressii was once much cultivated, and if lost should be reintroduced. From Victorian accounts it is as easy as the other species and will respond to the same methods. From Costa Rica, it has foliage and tubers similar to, but somewhat narrower than, *U. alpina*. Up to five large drooping flowers, pale lilac with yellow palates, are borne on a scape to 30cm (12in). *U. calycifida* from Venezuela, Guyana and Suriname has foliage similar to that of *U. longifolia*, but half the size. The scapes are up to 15cm (6in) long and bear several small mauve flowers. Use a 12.5cm (5in) pot.

One of the most beautiful species is *U. reniformis*, a native of Guyana and Venezuela. Variable in the wild, there seem to be at least two kinds in cultivation, a large and a smaller form. The larger is a splendid thing: the foliage itself is fine, a leaf consisting of a roundly kidney-shaped, almost glaucous-green blade to 7cm (2.75in) wide, which is thick and almost succulent and supported horizontally on an erect, reddish, wiry stem about 30cm (12in) high. The scape is up to 45cm (17.7in) across, of pale violet and with a balloon-like palate marked with two vertical lines of gold, edged in dark violet. Occasional potato-like ground tubers are produced. This plant needs room for its development, and grows well in a 30cm (12in) dwarf pot or orchid basket. The smaller form is about two-thirds its size, with light green foliage. The Brazilian *U. nephrophylla* may shortly be declared a form of the last species, which will be a pity, for there are differences in the live plant which are not apparent in the preserved material studied by botanists. The foliage is small, thin, almost membranous, the blade seldom more than 3cm (1.2in) in diameter, and short stalked, and in my plants there are no ground tubers. Although the flower is almost as large as that of *U. reniformis*, the inflated palate is, however, more pointed, and while the lower lip of the latter forms two distinct lobes, that of *U. nephrophylla* is more skirt-like.

U. nelumbifolia is native to the Organ Mountains in Brazil, and is of interest as one of the two species which is epiphytic not upon trees but in the water vessel of a giant terrestrial bromeliad (*Broccini* sp.). It has round blades up to 6cm (2.4in) tall, bearing up to three flowers 15mm (0.6in) long of pale pink to violet. From the base of the flowering stalk long runners are sent out which in nature may go for a considerable distance before they locate the water vessel of another *Brocchinia*, where it forms a new plant. Grow this in pure live sphagnum, but in every other respect treat as recommended for *U. reniformis*. Where *U. humboldtii* occurs on the Kaieteur savannah in Guyana it is found only in the water bowl of the trunk-forming bromeliad *Brocchinia cordylinoides*, which can reach 4.9m (14ft) in height, but in Venezuela at Mount Roraima it is found both in the *Brocchinia* and in wet mossy ground. It appears not to be in cultivation, though should succeed given the same treatment as *nelumbifolia*. The plant is rather similar, though the bladders can be as much as 6.25mm (0.25in) across, the flowers violet and said to be of an especially intense colour in the Roraima form.

The splendid vermilion-flowered *U. quelchii* has been seen and marvelled at by

Greater Bladderwort *U. vulgaris* flowers
above water

members of almost every expedition to Mount Roraima. It appears to produce tubers as insurance against drought, so there should be no difficulties in transporting it alive. Another worthy candidate is *U. campbelliana*, which clings to moss on trees in Venezuela and Guyana. Its leaves are tiny, but it produces large, brilliant-red flowers to about 2.7cm (1.1in) across.

SOME AQUATIC BLADDERWORTS

Few of the large number of aquatic species are in cultivation, and a large proportion of these are of North American and European origin. They are mostly characterized by long, underwater, free-floating and rootless stems bearing alternate, filamentous, bladder-bearing foliage. Some continue in growth throughout the year, but others die away for the winter, leaving only terminal 'resting buds' called turions, usually consisting of a little ball of thickly clustered juvenile foliage. These spend the winter at the bottom of the pool, rising with the spring to form new plants.

THE SPECIES

Of those that form winter turions the Greater Bladderwort *U. vulgaris* is surely the most exciting, for not only is it large in growth generally, including its traps, it also has great beauty in foliage and flower. Its wide distribution covers most of Europe (including Britain), temperate Asia and North Africa. The occasionally branching stems float below the water surface and can exceed 3m (9ft10in) in length; they are thickly clothed with fern-like, much-divided foliage which is thickly laden with bladders. These can exceed 5mm (0.2in) in length, and an idea of their catching capability can be gathered from material taken from a garden pond, which also gives a hint of their value to the plant. The several flowers are borne on long scapes rising up to 25cm (10in) above the water. They are up to 10mm (0.4in) wide and of rich yellow, and the palate is delicately pencilled in bright red.

The Popweed *U. macrorhiza* of the US could easily be mistaken for *U. vulgaris*, but has a hooked spur and much larger winter turions. The Western Bladderwort, as it is called, *U. australis* (syn. *U. neglecta*), though botanically distinct is very much like a smaller edition. One difference is that the upper lip projects beyond the palate, not the case in *U. vulgaris*. Its range is far reaching, being found through Europe to South Africa, through Asia to Japan, Australia, Tasmania and New Zealand. Again it is replaced in the US by a similar species, *U. geminoscapa*, the Hidden Fruited Bladderwort, which has a blunt palate and more slender scape. Much smaller, the Lesser Bladderwort *U. minor* occurs in Britain and Europe, North America and Asia. Its foliage seldom exceeds 6mm (0.25in) in length, and the traps are proportionately tiny. It favours very shallow peaty water, where much of the plant may be submerged in peat mud, and seems only to produce its flowering stems, bearing several pretty pale-yellow flowers, when drought threatens to dry its habitat.

From the south-eastern US comes the Swollen Bladderwort *U. inflata*, the underwater growth of which bears a superficial likeness to that of *U. vulgaris*. One obvious difference, however, is in the extraordinary flotation device for the scape. This consists of between five and ten narrow boat-shaped floats arranged radially, like the spokes of a wheel, at a point midway up the scape. They rise to the surface on becoming filled with air, and the top half of the scape then develops, bearing up to twelve bright-yellow flowers. This plant will also develop small seed-like tubers at the end of the stems in certain conditions (for example, when the water is low), which can withstand drought and form new plants. This species will form winter turions if exposed to low temperatures, but will otherwise remain in continuous growth. *U. radiata*, also from the US, has fewer floats and flowers and is a smaller plant. The Intermediate or Flat-Leaved Bladderwort *U. intermedia*, differs from all the foregoing in that its bladders are borne on colourless branching shoots, usually suspended into the mud, and which possess no foliage. These shoots arise from the main stems which bear awl-shaped foliage and no bladders. It bears flowering stems of up to six lemon-yellow flowers and occurs in the UK, Europe, the US and Asia. There is a very similar species, *U. ochroleuca*, which occurs less commonly in the US and on the European mainland. The more obvious differences are that the specialized bladder-bearing branches often bear some foliage, while the spur of the flower is pyramidal rather than cylindrical. The lovely Purple Bladderwort *U. purpurea* differs from all the above not only in the colour of its flowers, but because foliage is entirely absent. This is replaced along the main stem by whorls of six or seven much-divided filamentous shoots which bear the bladders. The scape bears several beautiful purple-pink flowers with paler, much-inflated palates. This species will produce winter turions if subjected to cold conditions, otherwise remaining in growth. It is found in easterly parts of Canada and the US, and also in Honduras and Cuba.

Of species that remain in continuous growth and never produce turions, *U. gibba* is a small grower and inhabits shallow acid waters in the US. Its foliage never exceeds 10mm (0.4in) in length, and the traps are tiny. The scapes are up to 7cm (2.75in), bearing up to three bright-yellow flowers. Like a miniature of this, at a third its size, is the diminutive *U. exoleta*, which occurs in Japan, Australia, Africa, Spain and Portugal. At the other extreme, the Twin-Flowered Bladderwort *U. biflora* is like is like giant edition of *U. gibba*, the flowers, usually borne in pairs, being over twice the size and the foliage branching twice, whereas in *U. gibba* it does so once only. It is native to North America, as is *U. fibrosa* which it much resembles. Differences are that the latter produces a few bladder-free branches and that the foliage on these branches thrice instead of twice, also that in place of twin flowers there are up to six per scape.

Decidedly different from any of these is the Twining Bladderwort *U. volubilis* from Western Australia, which is not free-floating and attaches itself in the mud beneath the water. The tufts of fine hair-like leaves are up to about 5cm (2in) long, and there are three different kinds of bladder trap, the largest of which can reach 5mm (0.2in) in length. The flowering scapes attach themselves to reeds and rushes by twining, and bear several fine purple flowers in pairs. These are large, to about 2.5cm (1in) across.

Cultivation All free-floating species may be cultivated under glass, and some are satisfactory indoors. All may also be grown out of doors in the right climates. With the exception of *U. volubilis* (see section below), they are easily propagated by division of the main growth or, in those species that form them, from turions.

Cultivation under glass In the house or greenhouse, they are best grown in peat-infused water. To prepare this, measure one-third of a teacupful of moss peat for every gallon of the capacity of the container you wish to use. Place the peat in a saucepan and put enough soft water in it to make a liquid 'soup'. Bring to the boil and simmer for about four minutes. Add this, including the peat, to the bulk of the water and do not add your plant until the water has cleared to a straw colour.

Choose your container to suit the growth of the species. A small goldfish bowl would be large enough to *U. gibba*, *U. exoleta* and *U. intermedia*, but one at least as large as 30 x 90 x 30cm (12 x 36 x 12in), or its equivalent in cubic capacity, but as deep, is necessary for such large growers as *U. inflata*, *U. vulgaris* and *U. purpurea*, while something in between will be adequate for *U. fibrosa* and *U. australis*. Indoors it favours glass containers, such as aquariums, which are best placed in north-facing windows. Do not anchor or 'plant' these free-floating species in any way – merely place them in the water. In the lighter conditions of the greenhouse, use black plastic or other opaque vessels to assist in cutting down the light. In all cases they should be protected from direct sunlight.

About two weeks later (not earlier, for their microscopic life must first be allowed time to develop), introduce water fleas (*Daphnia*, *Cyclops* or *Cypris*), as food for the plants. Live *Daphnia* can often be bought at pet shops and aquarium suppliers, but are easily introduced in the form of a jar of water taken from a clear and well-established pond which is not stocked with too many fish. It is not usually necessary to introduce them more than once, as they will normally maintain their numbers by breeding. The plants do not, as a rule, suffer from any pests or diseases, but green algae can be a problem and this can affect their growth. It can occur as filamentous algae, somewhat resembling green cotton wool, as single-celled microscopic algae which turn the water green, and as a floating scum. The scum can be removed by laying clean pieces of paper flat on the water surface; the algae cling to this and are thus removed with the paper.

Green water will be controlled by water fleas which eat the algae, and to some degree this can be the case with filamentous algae. But if filamentous algae become too much of a problem it may be necessary to gently wash the plants in a bowl of water, using a sable brush, and to prepare a new infusion. The formation of excessive algae growth is often caused by too much light, and if the container is placed in rather darker conditions the problem may not arise again, or you may cut it down by allowing Floating Fern (*Azolla caroliniana*) to form a blanket over no more than three-quarters of the surface.

Tropical free-floating species of *Utricularia* will almost certainly respond to exactly the same treatment, with the one difference: they will require the temperatures of the warmhouse or stovehouses.

Cultivation out of doors What species you can successfully grow in ponds out of doors will depend upon your climate, though otherwise there is little doubt that the requirements of all will be very similar, but with some needing deeper water than others. In the UK, *U. vulgaris* and *U. australis* are best grown in this way, though in starting it is a wise precaution to keep some growing indoors until you are sure that your outside material is firmly established, for they are vulnerable to beetle attack, against which I have found no answer. In nature, both are plants of acid water, but neither seems to object to moderately alkaline water in cultivation. Do not anchor the plants, since they are free-floaters. The water should not be less than 30cm (12in) deep for *U. australis*. They dislike being crowded by other pond weeds and, like all bladderworts, hate direct sunlight. This is easily cut out by the pads of water lilies. They are not likely to succeed in ponds overstocked with fish, for here food will be scarce, and they dislike being constantly pushed about. *U. minor* is an ideal subject for a shallow pool, ideally in 5–15cm (2–6in) of water. I grew it for many years in no more than 7.5cm (3in) of water in a tiny tub-pool in a little rock garden, in company with that delightful diminutive pygmy water lily *Nymphaea pygmaea alba*, which provided the shade it appreciates.

Cultivation of *U. volubilis* This is a self-anchoring species which requires different treatment. It is not always easy to re-establish, so be warned that if your plant has been out of water and exposed to the effects of drying for more than a few minutes, be it potted or bare-rooted, its foliage can be expected to first die away completely. Whether new growth then emerges or the plant perishes is a gamble, but one which is worth taking, so keep sprinkling your plant with water while it is exposed to air. Once you have established a clump, you will find it relatively undemanding.

Choose a black or dark-coloured container about the size of a small bucket (lighter colours will reflect the light, which is disadvantageous). Take a 15cm (6in) dwarf pot of the same colour, and fill this to within 12mm (0.5in) of the top with a well-dampened mixture of 3 parts moss peat to 1 part horticultural sand, which should be well compressed, and cover this to rim level with horticultural sand after having planted your bladderwort, so that the union of the foliage and basal growth is just beneath the surface level of the sand. The object of the layer of sand is to stabilize the peat. Air bubbles escaping from the peat can still do so.

Place the pot in the bucket or other deep container, and start to add soft water very gently, a little at a time, allowing time for each application to be absorbed, until the water is at the level of the surface of the sand. Allow it to be at this level for about five minutes before adding sufficient to bring it about one inch above this. After a couple of hours you may then bring the level to some six inches more. Boil a cupful of peat in a saucepan of soft water and simmer for four minutes. Make this up to half a gallon by adding it to soft water in a deep container, and stand until the peat is at the bottom and the water is clear. Decant the clear water into a can, and pour with the sprinkler into the bucket, throwing the peat deposit away (which must on no account be placed in the bucket). Make up the water-level to the top of the container, and shade.

The plant will ultimately benefit from the infusion, as will the microscopic life on which it will feed. After fourteen or more days, add water fleas (as for cultivation under glass). Support the twining, flowering stems with split bamboos. Your plant will gradually colonize the pot with runner stolons, and will itself eventually form a hefty clump. You may propagate by division, but do not do so until you have a colony. *U. hookeri* is likely to respond to the same methods.

The Pink Petticoats: Polypompholyx

At the time of writing it seems likely that botanists will place these terrestrial annuals with the bladderworts. The flowers are very different from those of any *Utricularia*. *Polypompholyx* have four calyx lobes and *Utricularia* have two. The traps differ significantly in design.

There are two species, *P. multifida* is the larger and is very free flowering. The erect, narrow scapes are up to 23cm (9in) long, and bear up to seven pretty rose-pink flowers with a yellow palate bordered in red. The scape rises from a cluster of foliage which is minute in comparison, but the system of underground bladders set with numerous traps is extensive. Native to Western Australia.

P. tenella is also found there, but occurs too in South Australia and Victoria. It is like a much smaller edition, with only one or two flowers to the scape. Both must be raised annually in the coolhouse, from seed sown on the surface of a compost of 3 parts moss peat to 1 part horticultural sand. A 12.5cm (5in) dwarf pot is suitable. Do not cover the seed. They like full sun, but light shading should be applied to the glass in summer. Water on the tray system.

The Waterwheel Plant: Aldrovanda

This strange little free-floating plant is closely related to the Venus Fly Trap. There is only one species in the genus, *A. vesiculosa*. The leaves are arranged in waterwheel-like whorls of eight, or occasionally six or nine, and each bears at its end a single trap which scarcely ever exceeds 2mm (0.08in) in length, and in structure and function is very similar to a Venus Fly Trap. Its prey consists of small swimming creatures, such as water fleas (*Daphnia*, *Cyclops*, etc.). Entirely rootless, the stem is up to 15cm (6in) long, though usually much shorter, its length tending to remain fairly constant, for as the tip grows so does the end die and disintegrate. Occasionally it branches, and in this way two plants are soon

A single open trap of *Aldrovanda*. The detached piece of stem explains why it is called the Waterwheel Plant formed. In summer small, solitary, five-petalled white flowers may appear just above the water surface. It has a wide distribution, occurring in various parts of Europe (excluding Britain), and in Africa eastwards through India and Japan to Australia. Choosy in habitat, it favours acid water where it likes to grow between the stems of reeds and rushes. It hates polluted waters, and is becoming ever rarer in Europe, due principally to the drain-off of chemicals widely used in agriculture.

Cultivation *Aldrovanda* will not tolerate direct sunlight, and will grow satisfactorily at the light level of the average room. In the greenhouse it should not only be grown in a sunless position, but every effort should be made to cut down light to the extent under which the plant thrives best. This may be done by placing the container under something that will cast more shade, such as a large, wide-spreading plant, or by floating on the surface under Floating Fern (*Azolla caroliniana*) to cover about two-thirds of it, though never more. For a growing tank in the greenhouse use a half-gallon (2.28 litres) rigid polythene ice-cream container. Prepare a peat infusion in precisely the same way as is recommended for aquatic *Utricularia* (see page 117), add to the bulk of the water and when the water is clear and straw-coloured add the plants. Add some water fleas after fourteen days.

The form in general cultivation at the present time is from sub-tropical Japan, and can be kept constantly in growth if kept to a minimum winter temperature of 18.5°C (65°F). It is also easily grown in the coolhouse, but here it will die back in autumn, overwintering as tight resting buds which rise and come into growth again in late spring. The peat-infused culture may support thriving plants for two or more years, but if they seem to lack their previous vigour it may be wise to prepare a fresh culture exactly as before.

Green algae can cause a problem, and if present in any quantity will affect the growth of the plants. For their control, see *Utricularia* on page 117 but never use an algicide, for copper is very poisonous to this species.

Propagation is simple. Cut in half any plant which is over 2.5cm (1in) in length. The half with the growing end intact will continue in growth, while the lower half will bud and so form a new plant.

The Tropical Pitcher Plants or Monkey Cups: Nepenthes

N. stenophylla has beautiful upper pitchers

This is a fascinating genus which finds its chief home in the Far East, centred on Borneo, but individual species are found in such far-flung places as Madagascar, northern India, Queensland and New Caledonia.

Of some seventy-three known species most are woody stemmed, climbing or scrambling, a few prostrate or shrubby. The leaf is usually narrowly lance-shaped and terminates in an often long tendril, at the end of which is, at first, a brown to green hook-like organ. It is from this that the pitcher will be formed, if at all, for by no means all leaves develop them. If this is to happen, the 'hook' will increase noticeably in size each day, until it resembles a perfect flattened but closed pitcher. Then suddenly it becomes inflated. Next the lid opens, when you will find that there is already digestive fluid in the pitcher bottom. Then a fold around the rim changes shape to become the ribbed peristome, and lastly the pitcher assumes its individual colours. This is a fascinating process.

In most species the mature plant bears two kinds of pitfall pitcher trap, which function in a way rather similar to those of *Sarracenia*. The lower pitcher is usually somewhat tub-shaped with two frontal wings which are fringed with bristle-like processes, and in the wild it always rests upon the ground. The tendril is usually attached to the pitcher at the front. The upper or aerial pitcher, on the other hand, is suspended in the air and has a longer tendril which gradually widens until it forms the base of the pitcher at the rear. The tendril also differs in forming a loop by which it can attach itself to vegetation for support.

The flowers are small and of a green, bronze or reddish hue, many being borne in a foxtail-like panicle or raceme. They are unisexual, those of one sex only being borne on one plant, and the flowers on the female plant must therefore be fertilized with pollen from the flowers of a separate male plant, to set seed.

General cultivation For horticultural purposes the species are divided into two groups; the lowland species, occurring in the wild at below 1,000m (3,300ft), and the highland species from above this elevation. Each needs rather different treatment as regards temperature, so ideally both should have their own glasshouses in which these conditions may be provided. But in practice, it is often possible to construct specially glazed partitions for them within the greenhouse, in which the appropriate heating is available. Alternatively, a number make ideal subjects for a heated terrarium, which must have a thermostat to ensure the individual temperature requirements of the type grown.

Temperature Lowland species require stovehouse temperatures. Unless you live in a very warm to tropical climate this will mean heating the greenhouse throughout the year. In summer the night minimum should be 21°C (70°F), but in the daytime one of 24°C (75°F) is preferable, and sunshine may be allowed to raise the temperature to as much as 38°C (100°F), but at this point the ventilators should be opened, and it is therefore wise to choose automatically controlled models. Ideally, the winter minimum should be not less than 18.5°C (65°F), but where fuel economy is important you may safely reduce this to 15.5°C (60°F). Joseph Mazrimas found it possible to let the temperature fall as low as 10°C

(50°F) at night in winter, if daytime temperature exceeded 27°C (80°F). Lowland hybrids have the same requirements, as have all those hybrids containing highland and lowland mixtures that I have come across.

Highland species will in few cases tolerate such temperature ranges; *NN. stenophylla, alata, tentaculata* and *gracillima* will grow well in them, but this is more a case of toleration than of requirement, and for the majority stovehouse temperatures cause ill health or death. They differ from the lowland species in not only experiencing lower day temperatures, but, more importantly, often considerably lower night temperatures. This wide fluctuation between the night and day extremes provides the key factor to their successful cultivation.

If you live in a cool climate you will need to provide some heating during cooler weather in summer, to maintain a daytime minimum of 18.5°C (65°F). Above 21°C (70°F) every effort must be made to keep the temperature down as much as possible, so at this temperature you should commence ventilation (automatically controlled vents are again a clear advantage), combining this with well damping down the floor and spraying the foliage with water. The subsequent evaporation will help to keep the house cool and humid.

It is wise to install an automatic spray system, especially if there is any chance of the house's being unattended at any time, as we shall discuss in more detail below. If you live in a warm to hot climate you are unlikely to succeed with the majority of highland species unless you install a thermostatically controlled air-cooling system. Even with ventilation combined with damping down, the day temperature in cooler climates can vary from around 22°C (72°C) to as much as 35°C (95°F) in summer, but this does not matter if the temperature is allowed to decline sufficiently at night. The best way of ensuring this is to ventilate well when the outside air has cooled, well damping down, and then shutting down the vents for the night if they are manually operated.

In winter the day temperature may be allowed to vary between 18°C and 22°C (64.5–72°F), falling to between 8.5°C and 12°C (47–54°F) at night. The above temperature requirements and attention to the plants may appear complicated, but are easily applied, and the heating costs for highland *Nepenthes* are much lower than for lowland species.

Heating Ideally the best system for the *Nepenthes* house is one of hot water pipes connected to a solid fuel, gas or oil-fired boiler exterior to the house. However, there are certain disadvantages to this, as explained earlier. Gas heaters using Propane or other gases non-toxic to plants may prove more practicable, but note that they will necessitate slight but continuous ventilation while in use, and that the resulting loss in humidity will demand vigilance in damping down – see the section on heating on page 17.

Composts Many composts have been successfully used. The most important consideration is that they must remain open and sharply drained. Simon Malcomber uses pure live sphagnum of a kind that remains compacted and resilient if squeezed. But such moss is not always easily available, and a good alternative is a mixture of 2 parts orchid bark, 2 parts horticultural Perlite, and 1 part moss peat, well mixed together. It is important not to exceed that proportion of peat, for too much tends to inhibit growth.

Potting Baskets, rather than pots, allow excess water to drain away quickly. These may be wooden orchid baskets, which lend themselves well to being suspended from the roof with wires, ordinary wire hanging baskets, or a special rigid plastic basket designed for planting water lilies. If there is room, plant rooted cuttings directly into a fairly large basket; if neglected, a small one can quickly dry out, and use of the larger size saves disturbing your plant by repotting for a much longer period. Alternatively, you may use a 15cm (6in) full-length pot when they have outgrown the basket. When using pots always place a few broken pot crocks in the bottom to facilitate fast drainage, concave side downwards. The roots are brittle, and planting should be secure rather than firm. Water well to settle the compost around them. Unless you are suspending the container from the roof it should be placed on a surface, such as slatted staging or an upturned flower pot, which will allow excess water to run quickly away.

Watering *Nepenthes* are odd amongst carnivorous plants in that they do not object to water containing lime, but if you do use it you must not use sphagnum as a potting material (to which lime is poisonous), or peat, which it rots down, causing root decay. The peat content in the compost can, however, be replaced with horticultural Perlite of as fine a grade as possible. Always water from the top, because the container must never be allowed to stand in water.

Humidity You should maintain a high humidity always, especially when temperatures are at their highest. In the terrarium this is easily done, providing it has a floor of wet sand and there is minimal or no ventilation. But in the greenhouse maintain this by a combination of damping down the floor and spraying with water, and by ventilating only when it becomes absolutely necessary. The floor of the house should be continuously wet to allow constant evaporation, and it is advisable to damp down several times a day in hot weather.

First lay a groundsheet of thick black polythene, overlaying this with 2.5cm (1in) of fine shingle or gravel, laying 60 x 60cm (2 x 2ft) concrete slabs as a stepping-stone path. The polythene prevents the gravel mixing with the soil underneath, and prevents weed growth, while the gravel retains moisture and thus greatly prolongs the intervals between necessary dampings-down. Traditionally the damping down of the floor surface is done with a coarse sprinkler, but this is unnecessary if an automatic spray system is installed (see below).

In the greenhouse the plants themselves should be sprayed several times a day, the object being to thoroughly wet the foliage. In the case of terrarium-grown plants this is not essential, though a light daily spray is beneficial. It is important to use soft water for this operation if you have used live sphagnum or peat in your compost. Otherwise you can use limey or hard water, but this often leaves a visible deposit on foliage. You may also use an automatic system of overhead mist sprayers. This can be connected to the water mains, but if the mains water is limey there will not only be the disadvantage just referred to, but you will be unable to grow lime-hating plants such as epiphytic bladderworts in the same greenhouse if exposed to spray.

The alternative is to use an electric pump in conjunction with a stored soft-water supply, which may be in the form of a large tank under the staging, fed from rainwater roof guttering. Before choosing your pump, check with the manufacturers of the misting system what water pressure will be required. The pump manufacturers will then be able to advise you on a suitable pump. Electrical parts and controls must not be exposed to the wet, so they must either be installed in an adjoining building or in a simple weather-proofed hutch. This also applies to the siting of the pump, unless it is of the submersible type or of a special design. The electrical installation must be carried out by, or approved by, a qualified electrician.

Automatic wet-leaf on-off switches intended for mist propagation are not suitable in the *Nepenthes* house since they result in over-frequent spraying. It is best either to switch on the pump manually, leaving it to run for a minute or so, or to use a time switch with provision for the maximum number of on/offs required per day.

Shading Most *Nepenthes* appreciate sun; indeed in most species lack of it results in reduction of the number of pitchers produced. But strong sunlight will yellow and often burn the leaves, and it is necessary to apply medium shading to the glass in late spring, only removing this when the power of the sun has lessened in late autumn. *N. ampullaria* and *N. rafflesiana* produce pitchers well and grow best in a light position in full shade.

Feeding Unlike most carnivorous plants, *Nepenthes* benefit greatly from feeding. This may be in the form of a high-nitrogen liquid feed applied to the roots weekly in summer, monthly in winter, or as a foliar feed at a quarter strength, applied to the foliage in a spray. Simon Malcomber uses Orchidquick at the rate of 10ml to 13.5litres (3gallons) of water, and applies this twice weekly in summer, once a week in winter.

Pruning Older plants should be pruned in early spring. In this way vigorous growth is maintained which is likely to bear plenty of pitchers. In the majority of species the most attractive are the lower pitchers, and these species should be pruned annually when sufficiently grown. Where the upper pitchers are the most desirable (e.g. in *N. khasiana*), it is best done biennially, for few if any will be produced in the first year after pruning. It should be severe: prune the main stems down to within about 5–15cm (2–6in) of the ground, depending on the size and growth of the plant, and leave a little green growth intact if possible. Even if you are only able to leave brown stems devoid of obvious growth, these almost invariably shoot within weeks, often in several places. Always use sharp secateurs. Healthy green growth once removed can be useful for cuttings.

PROPAGATION
This may be done by cuttings, layers and seed.

Cuttings are usually the best, for they will rapidly produce a good plant. They can be taken throughout the year, but those taken in the spring have the advantage of the full summer in which to develop into strong plants before winter.

Lowland species and hybrids are, as a rule, very easy indeed to strike, but with most highland species a 25 per cent strike is good, while *N. burbidgeae* is a definite candidate for layering. Plants raised from growth producing lower pitchers will form lower pitchers, ultimately followed by upper pitchers, but material taken from growth producing upper pitchers will only form upper pitchers. In most cases it is advisable therefore to take cuttings only from the former type, but where the main attraction is in the upper pitcher, as in *N. khasiana*, you may find the latter type preferable.

The cutting most likely to succeed will include the growing point of the shoot. It is possible to cut the remainder of the stem into cuttings at the same time (this is sensible when you have removed long lengths when pruning), but it is much better to wait until a shoot is produced, for it now has a much better chance of striking. Having taken this, wait for the other length to do likewise, and take another if you wish. Use a sharp knife and take your cuttings with a diagonal cut a little below the base of the leaf stalk.

Another type of cutting which is becoming popular with some growers is one taken with a heel. In this type the sideshoot is allowed to get long enough to form a cutting on its own. The main stem just below it is then severed and the shoot can be conveniently cut away with a heel, any loose bits being trimmed away to leave a cutting entirely of soft young growth, except for its shallow base.

As a precaution against rot, soak the cuttings for three minutes in a solution of Benomyl, a systemic fungicide. Allow this to dry, and then dip their bases into a suitable hormone rooting liquid. The best rooting medium is good quality live sphagnum moss, but failing this the previously recommended potting compost is satisfactory, as is horticultural vermiculite. Then insert the cuttings to about half their depth in small, full-length pots of appropriate size. Cuttings of lowland species and most hybrids are now best placed in a propagating case, to preserve high humidity, in a temperature of at least 21°C (70°F), and with a bottom heat, if possible, of 27°C (80°F), easily provided by a good electric propagator/terrarium. The medium should at all times be moist, though it must not be over watered, and the foliage should be wetted with a mist sprayer twice a day. Place in a light place but protect from direct sun. Rooting usually takes weeks but can take months. Keep the plant in the same pot until the need to transfer to a larger one is made obvious by its growth. Treat cuttings of the highland species identically, except that most will not stand the same high temperatures and bottom heat.

Layering Of the two kinds air layering is perhaps the most satisfactory. At a point 9–15cm (3.5–6in) down the stem and just below the base of a leaf stalk, a notch should be made by two cuts with a sharp knife to about half the depth of the stem. Apply a little rooting powder to this with a watercolour brush. Wash about half a handful of clean, live, good-quality sphagnum moss in soft water and squeezed out sufficiently to ensure that it is damp, rather than wet. Tie the moss in place around the stem, with a little cotton, making sure that the notch itself is filled with moss. Once it is in place, bandage it with thin plastic film (clingfilm is excellent) so that the moss is held firmly, rather than being loose or excessively tight. Seal it with tape at either end to prevent loss of water by evaporation, and shield the bandage from direct sunlight. Rooting should take place within weeks or, occasionally, months. After it has occurred remove the plastic covering, sever the stem just below the cutting and place in high humidity under a propagating cover for a few weeks to allow it to form a good root system.

A soil laying is notched and dusted with rooting hormone in a similar fashion, but is pegged down just under the surface of the compost in an adjacent pot.

Seed is easily germinated, providing it is fresh. The period of viability varies amongst the species. While *N. khasiana* will often germinate after a year's storage, in some species the period may not exceed ten days. Seed should, therefore, be sown the moment you receive it or, if that is not possible, it should be stored in the main compartment of the fridge.

Sow on the surface of a mixture of 3 parts moss peat to 1 part horticultural sand. It must not be buried. Wet the compost by placing the container in a tray of shallow soft water only until the surface is moist. Give it a light spray with Benomyl as a precaution against fungal attack. Then place the tray in a propagating case with a bottom heat of 27°C (80°F) in high humidity, which can be ensured if the sand bed is properly wetted. The position should be light but protected from direct sunlight. The air temperature should be at least 21°C (70°F). Germination usually occurs within six weeks' time, but can occasionally take much longer.

Lowland types can be left in the propagating case for an indefinite period after germination, before being moved to ordinary stovehouse conditions, for the bottom heat gives them an advantageous quick start. But the hot conditions and bottom heat will soon kill many highland species, so these should be removed as soon as a good proportion have germinated, and placed amongst the other highland species, covering the box with a propagator cover and protecting it from direct sunlight. When the foliage rosettes are about 2cm (0.78in) in diameter, or the seedlings have become clearly overcrowded, they should be pricked out. Use plastic boxes 9cm (3.5in) deep (cat-litter trays are good), liberally drilled with drainage holes on the bottom. Use the standard *Nepenthes* compost, but cover the surface with a 5mm (0.2in) layer of peat and sand in the 3 to 1 proportions, as this gives the seedlings an easier immediate roothold. Then dig up the seedlings taking care not to injure their roots, and gently prick out 3cm (1.1in) apart. Cover with a propagating dome to allow them to settle, placing the box in a sunless position. Remove after about a month. Spray lightly with a suitable fertilizer (e.g. Orchidquick), weekly in summer and fortnightly in winter. They can remain in the box until they appear to be getting overcrowded, when they should be transferred to 10cm (4in) pots, using the standard *Nepenthes* compost, and treated as adult plants.

If you have a male and a female plant in flower at the same time it is easy to produce your own seed. Unless both are of the same species – most unlikely – the pollination will produce hybrid offspring, and it is most important to keep a record of the parentage. Transfer pollen from the male flower to the female flower with a watercolour brush, and carry this out daily if you can. If you only have a male flower but it appears that you could have a female in flower within weeks, pollen can be stored for some weeks in the main compartment of the fridge. There is likely to be much variation among the seedlings. The ideal is to grow on as many as you have space for, ultimately retaining only the best in growth and pitcher and destroying all others.

Pests and diseases The damp atmosphere and conditions required by these plants tend to discourage bad attacks of many pests, but they do favour the development of fungal diseases which can affect both leaves and roots. To keep this at bay it is advisable to spray with fungicide once week. Try to avoid one which may be dangerous to the health if absorbed by the skin. Protective clothing should be used, and wash any part of exposed skin with soap immediately .

Aphis, whitefly and red spider can attack, but the worst offender is scale insect. All these have been disposed of with a good general systemic insecticide, such as Dimethoate, Malathion or other products which are special mixtures of these with HCH. In countries where these are not available, scale insect can be removed individually with an old toothbrush dipped in a solution of Malathion, while the other pests are more easily controlled by greenhouse insecticide sprays. Check with suppliers for the latest products.

THE SPECIES AND HYBRIDS

There are at least seventy-three known species, and the range of recorded hybrids is vast. To adequately describe the species alone would require a sizable monograph, so here my accounts are limited. For simplicity's sake many pitcher forms are illustrated in line drawings, rather than words (see page 135). These may also help to give some idea as to relative size, for they can vary so much in a single species that it is misleading to give their sizes in measurements. They can often vary considerably in shape and coloration within one species, and each description is of what the most commonly cultivated form.

LOWLAND SPECIES

Found almost exclusively under the altitude of 1,000m (3,300ft): In addition to those listed in the panel (left), there are a number of highland species which can descend below 1,000m in the wild, and which grow well in the conditions favoured by lowlanders, examples being *NN. alata*, *gracillima*, *gymnamphora*, *sanguinea*, and *madagascariensis*.

N. rafflesiana is the best all-rounder of the species. It is vigorous and easy to

LOWLAND SPECIES

NN. albomarginata, ampullaria, bellii, bicalcarata, campanulata, decurrens, x globamphora, gracilis, hamatus (dentate Kurata), *insignis, kampotiana, macrovulgaris, merrilliana, mirabilis, neglecta, neoguineensis, northiana, petiolata, rafflesiana, reinwardtiana, thorelii, tomoriana,* and *truncata*

'Cantley's Red' form of *N. ampullaria*

grow, beautiful in both its many lower and upper pitchers and produces abundant pitchers equally well in sun or in light shade. Although ultimately tall growing, it makes an excellent plant for the larger terrarium since it will withstand a lot of pruning, and when its growth becomes a problem it is easy to raise a new plant from a cutting.

The peristome rises abruptly at the back to form the tall stalk which supports the lid. This, with its double row of forward-pointing sharp ribs, is one of the chief characteristics of this species. The typical forms have pale-green pitchers richly spotted and speckled in dark crimson, but there are some equally desirable colour variants. Of these, var. *nigropurpurea* is predominantly darkest purple, with occasional green flecking on the pitcher and rather more green on the wings. It forms a perfect contrast to var. *nivea*, which has pitchers of the palest moonlight-cream. In var. *nivea elongata* the pitchers are of similar colour to the latter but twice as long.

Equally easy, *N. ampullaria*, with its quaint, unmistakable kettle-drum pitchers,

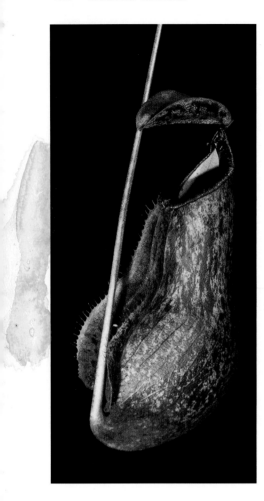

N. coccinea: pitchers of many hybrids acquire rich colours with age

is also an excellent terrarium plant, and produces pitchers in sunless conditions, which it seems to prefer. It is not a large grower. Since it does not produce upper pitchers at all, you need have no scruples in pruning it within reason. Unique in producing terrestrial pitchers which emerge from underground rhizomes, it needs to be grown in a large container. In other respects these pitchers are similar to the stem pitchers. There is a commonly grown all-green form, but in another the pitchers are pale green, beautifully speckled in red, reminding one of the eggs of many European wild birds.

Undoubtedly the most magnificent form is one discovered in a jungle in Brunei, North Borneo, by Robert Cantley. What appeared to be a group of toadstools from a distance proved on closer inspection to be a colony of *N. ampullaria*, the pitchers of which differed from all others in being of brilliant crimson-scarlet sparingly mottled in green. This is one of the most exciting and beautiful *Nepenthes* introductions. It is of one clone, and its discoverer has kindly allowed me to identify it with the varietal name of 'Cantley's Red'.

N. gracilis has rather narrow leaves and usually produces its small pitchers in abundance. There are many colour forms. The green ones are dull, but there are good red-spotted forms, others are of a pinkish hue, while there are fine forms with plum-maroon to blackish pitchers. *N. bicalcarata* is a vigorous, ultimately tall and large-leaved grower which is unique in having two tusk-like projections on the neck which supports the hood. This may possibly be used as a deterrent against the monkey-like *Tarsius* which raids the pitcher contents of some other species. The pitchers are suffused with orange. *N. reinwardtiana* is characterized by its slim and rather elegant form which hardly differs in the lower and upper pitchers. Usually green, clones exist in which they are tinted with mahogany. *N. mirabilis* is bewilderingly variable, with numerous geographical forms. The lower and upper pitchers are usually somewhat similar, with the oval lower part becoming cylindrical in the upper part, the mouth round, with a flattened peristome. Some easily cultivable, good forms are available. In one, the pitchers are green, in another they are so heavily dashed with colour as to appear completely red, and this is the one I recommend. In *N. albomarginata* the pitcher has a characteristic pure-white band on its outside, immediately beneath the peristome. There are green and pink-pitchered forms, the latter contrasting beautifully with the white band. *N. truncata* is unusual in having a short, somewhat spatula-shaped to nearly round, leaf blade. The pitchers are externally green, the lid suffused with red, and the upper surface of the inside is pale green, suffused and spotted with purple. *N. northiana* is remarkable for its fine peristome, which is wide and collar-like, the edges being somewhat scalloped. The pitcher is pale green, liberally spotted with purple, the peristome yellow striped with purple.

LOWLAND HYBRIDS
Most of these exemplify 'hybrid vigour', for they are generally more vigorous than many of the species, more inclined to form abundant pitchers, and easier to strike

 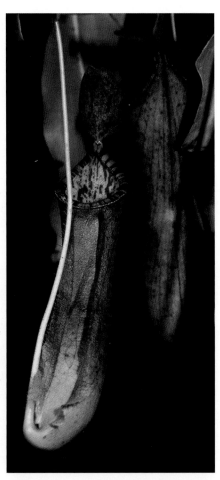

Far Left: Lower pitcher of *N. x mixta*
Left: Lower pitcher of *N. x* 'Ile de France'.

from cuttings. They are so numerous that only the best are listed here.

N. x hookeriana is the cross which occurs in the wild between *N. rafflesiana* and *N. ampullaria*. It is usually pale green with dark-red spots.

N. x mixta (northiana x maxima) is a fine plant in lower and upper pitcher. The steeply oblique peristome is wide, well ribbed and shiny, of beautiful ruby red, the pitchers green-spotted light purple, or, in var. *sanguinea*, reddish-brown blotched with chocolate.

N. x intermedia (gracilis x rafflesiana) inherits much of the neck of its paternal *N. rafflesiana*. The pitcher is light green, heavily dappled with red blotches.

In *N. x dyeriana (northiana x maxima* crossed with *rafflesiana x veitchii)* has cylindrically tub-shaped, yellow-green lower pitchers that are blotched and streaked bright red, contrasting with the coloration of the extremely wide

Above: *N. alata*

Right: Upper pitchers of *N. khasiana*

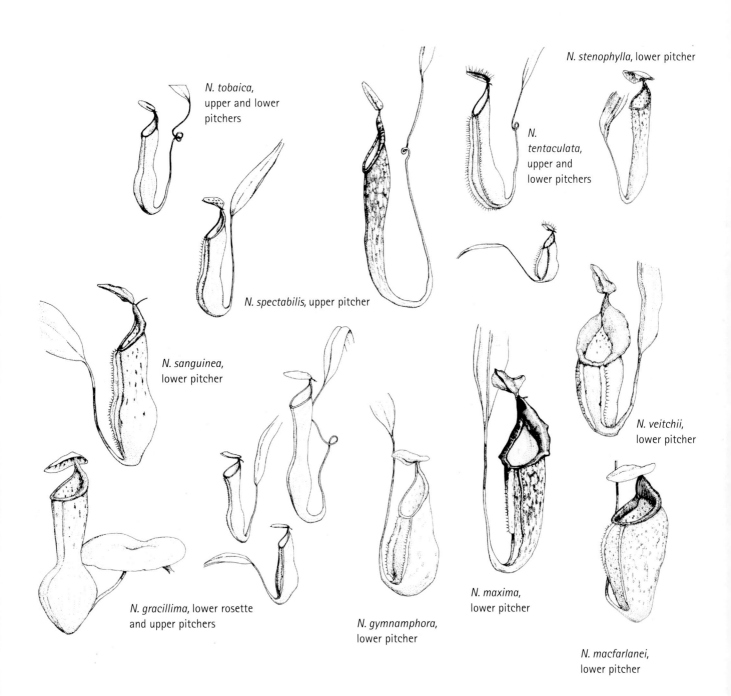

N. tobaica, upper and lower pitchers

N. stenophylla, lower pitcher

N. tentaculata, upper and lower pitchers

N. spectabilis, upper pitcher

N. sanguinea, lower pitcher

N. veitchii, lower pitcher

N. gracillima, lower rosette and upper pitchers

N. gymnamphora, lower pitcher

N. maxima, lower pitcher

N. macfarlanei, lower pitcher

N. tentaculata

peristome in creamy yellow-green, striped here and there in red.

N. x dormanniana (mirabilis crossed with *gracilis x khasiana)* has a light-green pitcher heavily blotched and spotted while the peristome and throat are green.

N. x wrigleyana (mirabilis crossed with *rafflesiana x ampullaria)* has pale-green pitchers heavily spotted in red.

In *N. x boissiense (gracilis x khasiana* crossed with *rafflesiana x ampullaria)* has pitchers of palest green with numerous small, light-crimson flecks and spots, while in *N. boissiense rubra* they are suffused with red. The plump-bellied *N. x morganiana (hookeriana x mirabilis)* has pale-green pitchers that are lightly and delicately flecked with red. Of the same parentage, *N. x lawrenciana* is very similar.

Family relationships have brought certain similarities of form to the following. *N. x chelsonii (rafflesiana x gracilis* crossed with *rafflesiana x ampullaria)* has light-green pitchers fairly heavily flecked red.

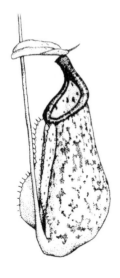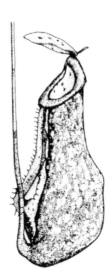

Left: Hybrid *N. x intermedia*

Below: *N. alata*

N. x coccinea (rafflesiana x ampullaria crossed with *mirabilis)* pitchers have much in common with *chelsonii,* but are covered with larger splodges and streaks.

N. x henreyana (gracilis x khasiana crossed with *rafflesiana x ampullaria)* has flecks of bright red that are so heavily applied that the appearance is that of a red pitcher lightly flecked with pale green. A separate seedling of the same parentage is *N. x williamsii,* which is of similar coloration.

N. x dominii (rafflesiana x gracilis) has light-green pitchers so heavily blotched with dark red as to be predominantly that colour, the cylindrical peristome contrasting with this in pale green. The back of the throat is pale green with purple spots, while the lid is green suffused with red.

N. x trichocarpa was, until recently, thought to be a species, but it has now been shown to be a naturally occurring hybrid between *N. gracilis* and *N. ampullaria.* It varies in coloration, but most people will find those with heavily red-spotted pitchers preferable to all others.

Of French hybrids, *N. x* 'Ile de France' (*x mixta sanguinea x kampotiana)* has lower pitchers with a pale-green base, the remainder being suffused with ruby pink often lightly streaked with dark red. It has a crimson peristome. The pitchers of *N. x* 'Ville de Rouen' are pale green suffused with pink and liberally streaked in red. The peristome is deep red.

HIGHLAND SPECIES
These occur at elevations above 1,000m (3,300ft). Most species are easy to grow, but when first potted they often prove to be more difficult to establish than their lowland relations. At this stage it is worth always ensuring the highest humidity by placing them under a propagating cover and by frequently spraying the foliage

N. burbidgeae from Borneo

with water. Their shyness to strike from cuttings makes them rather more expensive than one would wish.

There are two easy species which should be in every collection. *N. alata* is quite a small grower and is, therefore, excellent in the heated terrarium, and it is a prolific pitcher bearer. The lower and upper pitchers are very similar, and are narrowly cylindrical with a base that is globe-shaped in some forms, oval in others. There are many forms, most of which are worth growing, the coloration of the pitcher varying amongst these from green to those which are heavily suffused and streaked with red. Very different is the fast and tall growing *N. khasiana*.

The modest lower pitchers are green, slightly pink-suffused, but its chief glory is seen in the long and narrow upper pitchers which are richly variegated in red. Both will stand winter minimums down to 8°C (46°F). *N. khasiana* is also quite happy in the stovehouse, which *N. alata* will certainly tolerate, though it does better in cooler conditions.

N. ventricosa is a small grower which can bear generous quantities of pitchers. These may be light green flecked with red, to a pure creamy yellow-green in colour with red peristomes. In the closely related and rather similar *N. burkei* the pitchers are often suffused mahogany, which grows deeper with age.

N. gracillima is distinctive in its flat-fronted, narrowly cylindrical pitchers. They may be green heavily spotted with dark purple, or heavily suffused in purple, and Danser mentions a desirable form with white pitchers spotted in red. In the cylindrically pitchered *N. sanguinea* the coloration is deep red in the most desirable form, or green with red spots in a less-commonly cultivated form. The cylindrical lower pitchers and trumpet-shaped upper pitchers of *N. maxima* are equally attractive. Both are pale green, longitudinally flecked in dark red, and are notable for their fine peristomes, which are dark red, wide and scalloped. In *N. stenophylla* the small and narrow lower pitchers are fine, but the horn-shaped upper pitchers can be magnificent in form, coloration and size (they can reach 28cm (11in) in length). They are of the palest yellow-green, flecked and striped longitudinally with purple. These four species seem equally at home in the stovehouse as in typical highland conditions, and do best if the winter minimum does not fall below 13°C (55°F).

N. fusca is an easy grower, though it objects to high temperatures. The lower pitchers are small, the upper ones much larger with bell-mouths. The pitcher is mid-green streaked in crimson-maroon, while the narrow lid is dark maroon. *N. gymnamphora* has distinctively shaped pitchers which are generally green, much flecked with purple in the wild, but a form in which they are of the most lovely coral pink is in cultivation. In *N. macfarlanei* the oval lower pitchers are green to brownish green spotted with red, but the funnel-shaped upper pitchers are most often light green. The two frontal ribs are reddish, with red stripes on the peristome and red spots within the upper part of the pitcher. In *N. tobaica* the pitchers are commonly yellowish-green with red spots or flecks and a reddish peristome, but there are forms more heavily marked with, or almost entirely, red.

HIGHLAND SPECIES

NN. alata, anamensis, bongso, boschiana, burbidgeae, burkei, carnuculata, clipeata, deaniana, densiflora, dentate, distillatoria, dubai, edwardsiana, ephippiata, fusca, geoffrayi, gracillima, gymnamphora, hamatus (syn. dentate Kurata), hirsute, inermis, klossii, khasiana, leptochila, lowii, macfarlanei, madagascariensis, maxima, mollis, muluensis, paniculata, papuana, pectinata, pervillei (syn. Anurosperma pervillei), pilosa, rajah, rhombicaulis, sanguinea, singalana, spatulata, spectabilis, stenophylla, tentaculata, tobaica, treubina, veitchii, ventricosa, viellardii and villosa.

Lower pitchers of one of the best highland hybrids, *N. x mestersiana* var. *purpurea*

N. tentaculata is a delightful miniature with prostrate stems, small lance-shaped leaves and pitchers in perfect proportion. It makes an ideal subject for the heated terrarium, though it is an excellent greenhouse subject too. Its specific name refers to the extraordinarily long bristles or 'tentacles' standing upright on the upper surface of the lid. The lower pitcher is light green to white, heavily blotched and speckled with reddish purple, while the upper pitcher is purplish green to dark red.

Though epiphytic, *N. veitchii* responds to normal treatment in cultivation. Its cylindrical pale-green pitchers have deeply fringed wings, but the most noticeable characteristic is the shiny, conspicuously ribbed, canary-yellow peristome which is remarkably wide: it is a fine plant. *N. lowii* is perhaps the most peculiar of all species. The pitchers of the juvenile rosette (the shape before the climbing stem is formed) are rather small and cylindrical, with a pronounced peristome.

They are richly suffused with carmine and, though attractive, are unremarkable. By contrast, the pitchers of the climbing stem are extraordinary. Moreover, the large peristome of the lower pitcher is here completely lacking, and there is only a rim. The inner surface of the lid is covered with enormously long bristles. There is no distinction between upper and lower pitchers. Though at present rare in cultivation and difficult to propagate. This is one of the easiest species to grow.

Mount Kinabalu, in Borneo, is famous for its *Nepenthes* species, and the following four occur in no other place. *N. burbidgeae* must surely rank as one of the most beautiful in the genus, and the pitchers can be very large. Their background colour is palest green, in the best forms, to creamy white, and this is blotched and spotted with scarlet. The cylindrical peristome is creamy green striped with purple, while the large lid is pale yellow blotched with red. Easy to grow, it appears to be impossible from cuttings, but succeeds from air layers. The following two rarities are remarkable for their fine peristomes with large, widely spaced, disc-like ribs. *N. villosa* can be found at 3,200m (10,500ft) on the mountain, a higher elevation than any other species. The pot-shaped pitcher is soft yellow to yellowish-green, often tinted with red, the peristome ribs being yellow. It is now in cultivation and responds to normal highland treatment, as does its close relative *N. edwardsiana*. The latter differs in being a climber and in being usually epiphytic. The most obvious difference in the pitchers is that they are cylindrical. They are soft yellow to yellow-green, often beautifully suffused in scarlet, while the peristome is from yellow-green to, in the best forms, orange.

The king of monkey cups, *N. rajah*, sports the largest pitchers of any other in the genus. These can reach up to 35cm (14in) in length by 15cm (6in) in width, and they are also remarkable for the large size of their lids. Small wonder that in addition to its normal prey, small reptiles and mammals up to the size of, and including, rats can become accidental victims in nature! The pitcher is able to make full use of these, consuming almost everything save the bones. Once thought to be almost impossible to cultivate, it is not difficult to understand its likes and aversions. It hates direct sunlight, too low a humidity, and over-high temperatures. If you live in a warm or hot climate you are, therefore, unlikely to succeed without special air conditioning. Keep in a light place where it is shaded from direct sunlight. On Kinabalu the plant is a lover of waterfalls, often being found within their spray zone, and in cultivation it appreciates frequent spraying. High humidity is essential and a plant is best kept under a propagating dome to ensure this when it is young, later transferring it to a closed frame. Keep the greenhouse floor well damped down, especially in hot weather, being particularly careful to ventilate whenever the temperature reaches 21°C (70°F). Keep a watch for unhealthy foliage, and remove any that is dead. To avoid disease, spray with Captan weekly. Lastly, do not expect your plant to grow quickly, for this is essentially a slow grower.

N. dubai is graceful with unusual, yet dainty, upper pitchers. The closely related and very similar *N. inermis* has green, sometimes striped in brown, pitchers while

Upper pitchers of *N. ventricosa*. The form here is unusual in the waxy texture of its pitchers

there are reddish spots on the lid, but this differs in having no peristome. Both are from Sumatra, and I have adapted my drawings from Danser. From Borneo, *N. clipeata* is curious on account of its almost circular leaf blade, and the unusual form of the pitcher, which is olive-green flecked in red. A non-climbing, limestone cliff-dweller, it responds to normal treatment.

The first species to be discovered, in the seventeenth century, by the French was *N. madagascariensis*. The elegantly funnel-shaped upper pitchers are usually yellowish-green, while the hood and peristome are often blotched and tinted red. It is also of interest in being a native of Malagasy, which is some 6,000 miles west of the western limit of the main distribution zone of *Nepenthes* in the Far East. But it is not entirely isolated, for a short leap, geographically speaking, to the north-east are the Seychelles, where *N. pervillei* is found, notable for the distinctive form of its pitchers. The lower pitcher is usually green, the upper being often light mahogany, flecked in dark red. Though closely allied to *N. madagascariensis*, it differs triflingly from other species in the attachment of its seed. This has led some taxonomists to place it in a genus of its own, so that to our confusion we now have *Anurosperma pervillei* as one and the same plant.

HIGHLAND HYBRIDS

Few hybrids of highland parentage are in cultivation, yet as the price of fuel increases it seems important that we should move our attention towards breeding and growing these. Not only can they be expected to tolerate lower temperatures than the lowland hybrids, but the greater diversity of form and coloration of the highland species widens the possibilities in the range of hybrid offspring. Amongst those which have been raised, chiefly in Victorian times are the following, but the majority are either at present hidden away in widely scattered collections or, sadly, extinct: *NN. x allardii, x atropurpurea, x cylindrical, x excelsa, x* 'Dr John MacFarlane' *x mastersiana, x tiveyi, x ventrata, x wittei.* To these one may add two natural hybrids which await introduction, *N. x harryana (edwardsiana x villosa)* and *N. x kinabaluensis (rajah x villosa).*

Of those in general cultivation *N. x mastersiana (sanguinea x khasiana)* has fine cylindrical pitchers tinted with claret, this colour being especially deep in the var. *purpurea. N. x tiveyi (maxima superba x veitchii)* has particularly fine pitchers which are notable for their magnificent peristomes, which are like wide rolled-silk collars in mahogany red with scalloped edges. These contrast well with the pale-green pitchers which are lightly spotted red. *N. x ventrata (ventricosa x alata)* has liberally produced, bronzy-green pitchers similar in form to those of its *N. ventricosa* parent.

The Western Australian Pitcher Plant: Cephalotus

An easy and fascinating subject both for the cool greenhouse or indoors, *Cephalotus follicularis* is rare in nature, being found only in some bogs in the extreme south-western tip of Australia. There is only one species. The leaves are of two kinds, those which are shiny, flat, bright green, paddle-shaped and pointed, and the quaintly moccasin-like pitchers shown on the next page. Pitchers vary greatly in size. At their largest they may reach 5cm (2in) in length, but are usually considerably smaller, while those on the juvenile shoots (which established plants often produce) can be minute. The pitchers bear a superficial resemblance to those of the Monkey Cups, *Nepenthes* and, like them, hold a quantity of digestive fluid in the bottom part of the pitcher. Closer examination shows great structural differences in all parts of the plant, and it is clearly related to no other known carnivorous plant. It will produce flower stalks to as much as 60cm (12in) high, bearing numerous small greenish flowers which are singularly unattractive. Remove these scapes the moment they appear, for they sap some of the vigour of the plant.

Cultivation There appears to be no noticeable difference in growth between plants grown in compost and others grown in 3 parts moss peat to 1 part horticultural sand. They appreciate room for their roots, and can grow in a 12.5cm (5in) pot or in a wide container. Though they can be grown in a fairly low humidity, the pitcher size is greatly increased in a high one, and this is one of the few plants which is best placed under a propagating cover. It will do well in a sunny window or in a cool greenhouse exposed to sun, when the pitchers are more deeply coloured. This is one of the few carnivorous plants which will do well on a north-facing window-sill. Water on the tray system in summer, unless you are covering your plant with a propagator, when it is only necessary to ensure that the compost is always wet. In winter keep it a little drier but still moist, and only put sufficient soft water in a tray or saucer for the pot to fully absorb.

A curious phenomenon is that both in cultivation and the wild individual shoots will sometimes die back for no apparent reason, and you may think you have lost your plant. Providing there is a good root system this is seldom so. Merely cut off the dead part without disturbing the root system and new shoots almost invariably make their way to the surface, even though they may take up to eight weeks to do so. My plants suffer little from the attacks of pests and diseases. Greenfly can be harmful, but are easily controlled with any houseplant aphicide. Grey Moult (*Botrytis cinerea*) can spread from dead leaves and pitchers to the live plant, but should be no problem if all dead growth is routinely removed.

Propagation The best methods of increase are division, rhizome cuttings and leaf cuttings. Seed is sparsely produced and too slow a method to be recommended. Of these, the simplest is that of division of the rootstocks. Wait until your plant has not only produced a good clump but is producing growths elsewhere in the pot from underground stolons, and divide in early summer. Pot into a 12.5cm (5in) pot if the crown is of a mature size, but if smaller a 10cm (4in) pot will suffice, potting into the larger size when the plant has reached maturity.

Rhizome cuttings are also best taken in early summer, so the operation is best combined with division. Unpot, shake out loose compost and wash away the remainder from the roots, when you will be able to select the best material. A rhizome is an underground stem and is easily identified when young as it has scale-like bracts, which are whitish in this species. Later they die and become brown, but are retained until they rot away. The older rhizomes become thick, brown and root-like, and these are the ones that make the best cuttings. In selecting your material, remember that the parent plant must be left with a

The Western Australian pitcher plant, *Cephalotus follicularis*. In the centre is an 'ordinary' leaf sufficient root system so as not to impair its health. Cut off lengths of rhizome with a sharp knife with straight, clean, cross cuts. Cut these into lengths between 12–25mm (0.5–1in) long. Fill a 12.5cm (5in) dwarf pot to within 12mm (0.5in) of the top with the compost, firming this, and lay the cuttings flat, spacing them out so that they are not in contact with one another. Now cover them with compost so that they are no more than 6mm (0.25in) deep, and gently firm. Treat as you would the mature plant. After about eight weeks, shoots will appear regularly. When you are sure that all have emerged, and they have formed nice little plants, they may be potted separately into 10cm (4in) pots. Cuttings from the thick succulent roots of older plants can also be taken in exactly the same way.

Leaf cuttings may be taken from early to high summer. Both the 'ordinary' leaves and the pitcher leaves are suitable, but in both cases the entire stalk must be included, and it should be removed with as much base intact as possible. Fill a 12.5cm (5in) dwarf pot to within 6mm (0.25in) of the top with the compost, firming this and making it level. The leaf cuttings may be placed directly upon this, but if you have some live green sphagnum it is best to first cover the compost with the thinnest possible layer of finely broken sphagnum and to place them on this. In either case the pitcher leaves should be propped so that they are upright; place each in a small dent made in the surface. In both kinds of cutting the base of the stalk alone should be just covered with a speck of compost or broken sphagnum, the remainder of the leaf being uncovered. 'Ordinary' leaves are laid flat. Now soak the base of the pot in shallow soft water until the compost surface is moist, give the lightest sprinkling from above with the fine sprinkler of the watering-can to settle, remove from the water and place the pot in a light part of the coolhouse or indoors, but out of direct sunlight. Cover with a propagating dome to preserve high humidity. Over 50 per cent of the cuttings will usually strike, taking six weeks or longer to do so. Keep a constant check for rotten or mouldy leaves, and remove these at once, for infection spreads quickly. Do not pot up the small plants until they are a manageable size; they can be left for months in the pot. The growth of sphagnum moss may threaten to smother them, but this can be occasionally clipped with scissors.

Brocchinia

A carnivore, *Brocchinia reducta*

South America is well known for its bromeliads. A large number of these attach their neat rosettes to the trunks and twigs of trees, but not all are epiphytic, for a fair proportion are terrestrial species which are found in poor soils. In both types many have their leaf bases tightly pressed together to form what are called tanks. These are vase-like structures where rain collects, in the centre of the rosette. During short dry periods these provide the plant with water, but

PESTS AND DISEASES

Botrytis, seedling and cutting diseases
general fungal diseases
seed pests and diseases
caterpillars
tarsonemid mite
scale, mealy bug, red spider mite, whitefly
and aphis
leatherjackets, millipedes and other soil
pests
slugs, snails, woodlice

undoubtedly nutrients produced by the rotting down of detritus and insects, and so on, which happen to fall into the tank are of use to the plant. But are such plants really carnivorous? In the majority of cases the answer is certainly 'no', for careful examination has shown no signs of adaptations which are specialized to this purpose. It is clear that the small creatures are caught by accident rather than by design, and even though they will be of some slight benefit to the plant, the latter cannot be called carnivorous. This is certainly the case with most species in the genus *Brocchinia*, but one surprising exception was identified from material gathered by Professor Thomas J. Givnish in 1980.

NECTAR-SEEKERS

B. reducta grows in the Guayana Highlands in south-east Venezuela and adjacent Guyana, where it favours sterile, highly acid, sandy soils in bogs and wet savannahs. The narrow upright leaves are bright yellowish-green, around 33cm (13in) high. They are held tightly together in a cylindrical rosette, the lower part of the cylinder forming the vase in which rainwater collects. As in *Sarracenia flava*, the bright coloration is likely to prove an advertisement to flying nectar-seekers, as is the strong scent of honey given off by a substance released into the water by glands in the leaf bases. But this is a case of flagrant deception, for visitors entering the cylinder will find none. The inner surface of the leaves on which they find themselves is covered with wax which breaks off easily, giving an unsound foothold. A high proportion of such creatures are thus precipitated down into the water tank, where they drown.

As in *Darlingtonia* and *Heliamphora* there are no digestive glands, the soft parts of the bodies being broken down by bacteria. The leaf bases are scattered with microscopic gland-like structures called trichomes, and these absorb the resulting nutrients into the plant's system.

Judging from its natural habitat, in cultivation it will prefer a warm greenhouse, but is likely to grow satisfactorily in coolhouse conditions. Since it grows quite near to *Heliamphora heterodixa* it should appreciate frequent sprayings with soft water, but it is doubtful that it would favour being watered by the tray system, which does not suit other bromeliads. It will require a high humidity. Try a medium of 2 parts moss peat to 1 part horticultural sand, and use a 12.5cm (5in) pot, placing three broken crocks over the drainage hole, concave side downwards, before filling.

CHEMICALS FOR THE PROTECTION OF CARNIVOROUS PLANTS

The chemicals mentioned at the time of writing this book are currently available to the amateur. It is essential that the directions on the label of any product are followed for health and safety reasons, and also for efficient control of the plant's problem, in order to incur the minimum of damage. Active ingredients, products and product suppliers change and vary from country to country.

Store garden chemicals safely out of the sight and reach of children and pets, away from food and in a frost-free place.

Glossary

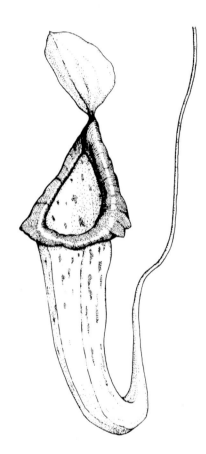

Anther
End part of stamen which bears the pollen.

Bracts
Small modified leaves often found at base of, or along, flowering stems, and sometimes near or on the calyx, as in *Sarracenia*.

Chlorophyll
The green colouring matter of plants which enables them to manufacture carbohydrates from carbon dioxide and water, by using energy derived from sunlight.

Clone
All plants obtained by vegetative propagation from one seedling are said to be of the same clone.

Column
The neck-like portion of the lowest part of the hood in many *Sarracenias*.

Compost
In this book used to mean a potting mixture usually containing two or more of the following: peat, sand, Perlite, sphagnum moss, pine bark, loam.

Corolla
The collective name for the petals of one flower.

Crocks
Pieces of broken clay plant pot sometimes placed in the bottom of a plant pot to improve drainage, the largest covering the drainage hole, the smaller ones on top, the concave sides downwards.

Decumbent
Lying on the ground, but with the apex or tip turning upwards.

Dichotomous
Repeatedly dividing into two branches.

Enzymes
Substances produced by and found in living cells. They are also found in digestive juices of animals and carnivorous plants, each having the power to break down specific substances.

Epiphyte (adj. **epiphytic**)
A plant that grows on another plant but is not a parasite.

Form
A plant displaying an inherited characteristic differing from the typical species or variety. However, it is not sufficiently stable or marked to justify the rank of variety.

Gemma (pl. *gemmae*)
A small body produced by the parent plant by non-sexual means which, when detached, may form a new individual.

Genus (pl. *genera*)
A category of closely related species; the generic name is given as the first of the two names of each species.

Gland
A structure of one or many cells which secretes a substance.

Hibernaculum (pl. *hibernacula*)
A winter resting bud formed when the main plant dies back, and from which the plant regenerates in suitable conditions. It is often rootless.

Hood
Lid-like appendage hanging over or above the opening of many pitcher leaves.

Inflorescence
Flowering branch or flowering part of the plant above the stem-leaves. Includes branches, bracts and flowers.

Interspecific cross
A hybrid between two species, sometimes termed an interspecies.

Linear leaf
A narrow leaf with near-parallel sides.

Loam
A well-balanced soil in which neither sand nor clay content predominates. The finest consists of good medium field topsoil that has been stacked for a year (to allow the turf to rot) and then riddled.

Midrib
The main vein of a leaf running centrally and longitudinally through the blade.

Mucilage
Glue-like compounds of vegetable origin and complex structure.

Ovary
Container in which seeds are formed.

Panicle
A branched raceme.

Pedicel
A stalk that is the last branch of an inflorescence, bearing the flower or fruit.

Peltate
A leaf or other flattened structure with the is attached to the lower surface.

Peristome
In *Nepenthes*, a plate inserted on the rim of the mouth in most species. It is down-curved on both sides, semicylindrical in section, and ribbed, the ribs being usually sharply toothed on the inner margin.

Petiole
The leaf stalk.

pH
A logarithmic index for the concentration of hydrogen ions in a solution. A
  reading below pH 7.0 indicates acidity; one above pH 7.0 indicates alkalinity.
Photosynthesis
The synthesis by plants of carbohydrates and more complex substances from
  carbon dioxide and water, using the energy from light through the agency of
  chlorophyll.
Phyllode (pl. *phyllodia*)
Leaf-like structures. In *Sarracenia* these are predominantly widened petioles.
Pistil
The female part of a flower comprising the ovary, style and stigma.
Protozoa (sing. *protozoan*)
Single-celled microscopic animals found in great numbers in both salt and fresh
  water, and in damp soil.
Raceme
An inflorescence consisting of a single main stem along which the flowers are
  borne on pedicels.
Reflexed
Turned backwards abruptly.
Rhizome
An underground root-like stem bearing scale-leaves and at least one bud.
Scale, scale-leaf
A leaf greatly reduced in size, and scale-like; usually sessile (see below) and seldom
  green.
Scape
A leafless flowering stem extending from a rosette of leaves or root to the flower
  or inflorescence.
Sepal
One of the leaf-like or petal-like members which make up the calyx of the flower.
Sessile
Attached without a stalk.
Species
A group of mutually fertile and closely allied plants displaying differences from
  other related plants.
Stamen
Part of the flower which produces pollen, usually consisting of a filament that
  bears the anther.
Stigma
The end of the style to which pollen must be transferred in order to germinate
  and bring about fertilization.
Stipule
One of the two leaf-like appendages that are often present at the base of the
  petiole.

Stolon
In *Utricularia* this refers to the underground stems of terrestrial and epiphytic
    species.
Style
The part of the pistil between the ovary and stigma.
Tuber
A swollen underground stem, or occasionally a root, used to store food material.
Turion
The hibernaculum or winter resting bud containing food, formed by many water
    plants including some of the aquatic *Utricularia* species.
Variety
A large number of individuals which differ from others in that species, and breed
    true from seed.
Venation
The veins of an organ as a whole, or their arrangement.
Whorl
A group in which identical organs (e.g. leaves) are arranged around the stem in a
    circle.

Nurseries, plant stockists and materials

Wherever possible order plants and materials from firms in your own country, since there is always a risk of delay in packages sent from abroad – a risk which all keen collectors will take when pursuing the occasional rarity. In some countries, import restrictions are severe, but there is seldom any restriction on the importation of seed; check in advance of ordering. There are numerous websites, many with on-line shops. The International Carnivorous Plant Society website has a web ring.

Bridgemere Garden World
near Nantwich
Cheshire CW5 7QB, UK
T: 01270 521100
E: info@bridgemere.co.uk
W: www.bridgemere.co.uk

Borneo Exotics
P.O. Box 2
Thalawathugoda
Sri Lanka
T: 94 (0) 114 307 287
F 94 (0) 114 307 287 ext 1
E: nepenthes@borneoexotics.com
W: www.borneoexotics.com

Bug Biting Plants
BugBitingPlants.com
1102 E 31st Street Apt D3
Brooklyn, New York 11210
Plants grown and shipped from the West
Coast, USA.
T: 347-312-2130
W: www.bugbitingplants.com

Burnham Nurseries Ltd
Forches Cross
Newton Abbot
Devon TQ12 6PZ, UK
T: 01626 352233
F: 01626 362167
E: mail@orchids.uk.com
W: www.orchids.uk.com

California Carnivores
2833 Old Gravenstein Highway South
Sebastopol
California 95472, USA
T: (707) 824-0433
F: (707) 824-2839
E: CALIFCARN@aol.com
W:www.californiacarnivores.com

Chiltern Seeds
Bortree Stile
Ulverston
Cumbria LA12 7PB, UK
(Seed only.)
T: 01229 581137
F:01229 584549
E: info@chilternseeds.co.uk
W: www.chilternseeds.co.uk

Cook's Carnivorous Plants
PO Box 2594
Eugene
OR 97402, USA
T: (541) 688-9426
W: www.flytraps.com

Easy Carnivores
P.O. Box 107
Pontefract
West Yorkshire
WF9 1YW, UK
T: 01977 651187
W: www.easycarnivores.co.uk

Exotica Plants
CMB Cordalba via Childers,
QLD 4660 , Australia
T: (07) 41 266 434
F: (07) 41 266 434
E: info@exoticaplants.com.au
W: www.exoticaplants.com.au

Flytraps4u, USA
W: www.flytraps4u.com

Hampshire Carnivorous Plants
Ya Mayla
Allington Lane
West End
Southampton SO30 3HQ, UK
T: +44 (0) 23 80 473314
F: +44 (0) 23 80 466080
E: matthew@msoper.freeserve.co.uk
W: www.hantsflytrap.com

Hungry Plants, South Africa
T: (+27) 083 514 0709
E: info@hungryplants.com
W: www.hungryplants.com

Lee's Botanical Gardens
P.O. Box 669
LaBelle
Florida 33975, USA
E: Buellmyster@olsusa.com
W: www.lbg-cp.com

Marcel Lecoufle
5 Rue de Paris
94470 Boissy-St-Lèger, France
T: 01-45-69-12-79

Mean Plants, USA
E: info@meanplants.com
W: www.meanplants.com

Peter Pauls Nurseries
2659 St. Rt. 21
Canandaigua
NY 14424-8713, USA
T: 585-394-7397
F: 585-394-4122
E: info@peterpauls.com
W: www.peterpauls.com

Shinya Yamada
E: s-yamada@hbs.ne.jp
W: www.hbs.ne.jp/home/s-yamada

South West Carnivorous Plants
2 Rose Cottages
Culmstock
Cullompton
Devon EX15 3JJ, UK
T: 01884 841549
E: flytraps@littleshopofhorrors.co.uk
W: www.littleshopofhorrors.co.uk

Trev Cox
Glanroon
Kilrohane
Co. Cork, Ireland
E: vortex@utvinternet.com
W: www.freewebs.com/vftshop

Triffid Nurseries
22 Glanville Road
Tavistock
Devon
PL19 0EB, UK
T: 01822 616871
E: andy@triffidnurseries.co.uk
W: www.triffidnurseries.co.uk

Triffid Park
257 Perry Road
Keysborough
Vic 3173, Australia
By appointment only.
T: 61 (0)3 9769 1663
F: 61 (0)3 9769 1663
E: Donna at triffids@triffidpark.com.au
W: www.triffidpark.com.au

Wistuba – Exotische Pflanzen
Mudauer Ring 227
68259 Mannheim
Germany
F: +49 621 7152028
E: nepenthes@wistuba.com
W: www.wistuba.com

Societies

Enthusiasts who have built up some sort of collection will find great advantages in joining a society. In addition to websites and journals, most offer other advantages such as seed and plant exchanges, talks and meetings. In addition to joining a national or local society membership of the International Carnivorous Plant Society is worthwhile. Truly international, it is an excellent way of getting in touch with other members in many parts of the world who are often interested in plant exchanges. Also see the website www.sarracenia.com/faq/faq6100 for others.

Association Française des Amateurs de
    Plantes Carnivores, Dionée
Association Dionée
Jardin Botanique de Lyon
Parc de la Tête d'Or
69459 Lyon, Cédex 06, France
E: bureau@dionee.org
W: dionée.nuxit.net

Australian Carnivorous Plant Society
    Inc.
9 Ryan Ave
Woodville West SA 5011, Australia
E: secretary@acps.org.au
W: www.acps.org.au

Australasian Carnivorous Plant Society
PO Box 4009
Kingsway West
NSW 2208, Australia
E: enquiries@auscps.com
W: www.auscps.com

The Carnivorous Plant Society
14 Rope Walk
Martock
Somerset TA12 6HZ
UK
E: UKCPS@aol.com
W: www.thecps.org.uk

Darwiniana
Zdenek Zacek
Ustavni 139
Praha 8
181 00, Czech Republic
E: ZZacek@seznam.cz

Drosera V.Z.W.
Marc Verdyck
Botanical garden, University of Gent
K.L. Ledeganckstraat 35
B-9000 Gent
E: verdyckmarc@freegates.be

Gesellchaft für Fleischfressende
    Pflanzen im deutschsprachigen Raum
    e.V.
Radolfzellerstr. 22
D-78467 Konstanz, Germany
E: vorsitzender@carnivoren.org
W: www.carnivoren.org

The International Carnivorous Plant
    Society, Inc.
PMB 322
1564-A Fitzgerald Drive
Pinole
California 94564-2229, USA
W: www.carnivorousplants.org

Japanese Carnivorous Plant Society
Naoki Tanabe
1-4-6 Minami Hanazono
Hanamigawa-Ku
Chiba City, Chiba Pref, 262-0022 Japan
E: jcpstanabe@msn.com
W: member.nifty.ne.jp/jcpstanabe

New Zealand Carnivorous Plant
    Society
PO Box 62007
Mount Wellington
Auckland, New Zealand
W: www.math.auckland.ac.nz

Vancouver Carnivorous Plant Club
6011 No. 7 Road
Richmond, British Columbia
Canada V6W 1E8
E: cteichreb@hotmail.com
W: www.geocities.com/vcpc2000

Victorian Carnivorous Plant Society,
    Inc.
PO Box 201
South Yarra
Victoria 3141, Australia
F: (03) 5634 2070
E: mail@vcps.au.com
W: www.vcps.au.com

Index

Picture Credits

Robert Cantley: *N. stenophylla*, Martin Cheek: *Sarracenia purpurea purpurea*, Jane Gate: *D. rotundifolia; S. flava, S. x excellens*. Marcel Lecoufle: *N.* x 'Ile de France'; x2 *N.* x coccinea. Paul Temple: *D. whittakeri*. Organics Image Library: front cover. Oxford Scientific Films: *Aldrovanda* trap

All other photographs: Adrian Slack
Line drawings: Adrian Slack